Woman
HEAL THY SOUL

Becoming Unstoppable:
Reawaken Your Resilience, Courage, and Strength

**SHAMEKA L. JONES, DR. JANELL JONES,
KRYSTAL A. EDWARDS, DR. CANDICE P. PARKER,
KEOSHA S. EDWARDS, SHERITA A. RILEY**

Copyright © 2024 by Melanin Grace Publishing in collaboration with Woman Heal Thy Soul

All rights reserved. No part of this publication may be reproduced, distributed, or transmitted in any form or by any means, including photocopying, recording, or other electronic or mechanical methods, without the prior written permission of the publisher, except in the case of brief quotations embodied in critical reviews and certain other noncommercial uses permitted by copyright law. For permission requests, write to the publisher, addressed "Attention: Permissions Coordinator," at the address below.

Melanin Grace Publishing
P.O. Box #721

Pickerington, Ohio 43147

Email: info@melaningracepublishing.com or info@womanhealthysoul.com

Disclaimer: This book is intended for general informational purposes only and does not provide medical or therapeutic advice. The contents are not intended to diagnose, treat, cure, or prevent any diseases or health conditions. The reader is encouraged to consult with a qualified healthcare professional before making any health-related decisions. The authors and publishers are not responsible for any specific health or allergy needs that may require medical supervision and are not liable for any damages or negative consequences from any treatment, action, application, or preparation, to any person reading or following the information in this book.

ISBN: 978-1-7369879-1-9 (paperback)
ISBN: 978-1-7336439-3-1 (ebook)

Dedication

To all the women who have faced adversity, low self-esteem, feelings of unworthiness, disappointment, and unfulfillment. To those who have struggled with self-doubt, societal pressures, and personal challenges. To the resilient souls who have endured heartbreak, injustice, and obstacles along their path.

This book is dedicated to your journey.

You possess an inner strength that can overcome any barrier. You have the power to rewrite your story and unlock your brilliant future. May these pages inspire you to embrace your worth, pursue your dreams, and shine your radiant light upon the world.

You are enough. You are capable. You are powerful beyond measure.

Table of Contents

Introduction 1

Hijacked by Shame and Guilt: Reclaiming
Perseverance: *Keosha S. Edwards* 5

Breaking Chains: The Journey to Self-Forgiveness and
Freedom: *Dr. Candice P. Parker* 17

Heartstrings of Healing: A Chronicle of Self-Love and
Self-Talk": *Sherita A. Riley* 37

Embracing the Journey of Self-Discovery: From
Limitations to Limitlessness: *Krystal A. Edwards* 49

Awakening The Inner Self: The Healing Power
of Mindfulness: *Shameka L. Jones* 67

Thriving Through Tears: A Guide to Overcoming
Grief: *Dr. Janell Jones* 83

About the Authors 101

An Exclusive Offering 116

Resources 118

Introduction

Welcome to "Woman Heal Thy Soul: Becoming Unstoppable: Reawaken Your Resilience, Courage, and Strength." This book is more than just a collection of pages; it's a beacon of hope and a guide for every woman ready to step out from the shadows of past traumas and into the light of her true potential.

The Burden of the Past

Do you ever feel burdened by the past? Its traumas may weave themselves into the fabric of your future, casting long shadows of shame, unforgiveness, and self-doubt. If you find yourself wrestling with feelings of inadequacy, battling the fear of rejection, or struggling to assert your needs and desires in a world that often demands you put yourself last, this book is for you.

A Sanctuary for Healing

Have you ever stood before the mirror, questioning your worth, purpose, or your true ability to be happy? If your heart whispers "yes" to any of these questions, you've found your sanctuary. Many women carry the scars of their battles in silence, allowing these wounds to dictate their self-worth and limit their vision of what's possible. "Woman Heal Thy Soul" invites you to turn the page on this narrative and embark on a journey of self-discovery, empowerment, and healing.

A Collective Cry for Freedom

This book is a collective outcry and celebration of women who've decided to stand tall, confront their demons, and reclaim their light. Authored by six courageous women, each story serves as a testament to the strength that lies within us all to overcome adversity and flourish. These narratives are not just stories; they are lifelines, extending a hand to you, the reader, guiding you through the darkness toward a place of self-love, understanding, and empowerment.

What to Expect

As you immerse yourself in these pages, imagine sitting alongside these remarkable women as they share their most vulnerable moments, their battles, and their victories. Their experiences offer invaluable insights into overcoming shame,

INTRODUCTION

embracing self-discovery, nurturing self-love, elevating self-esteem, mastering the art of forgiveness, and using mindfulness to become the best version of yourself.

The Journey Ahead

This book acknowledges the complexity of feelings and experiences that can hold us back—resentment, loneliness, jealousy, and the insidious grip of impostor syndrome. Yet, it also serves as a powerful declaration: it's time to break free from these chains. "Woman Heal Thy Soul" is not just about reading; it's about experiencing a metamorphosis, challenging yourself to ask the hard questions, and engaging in the deep, sometimes painful work of healing and becoming whole.

Embrace this journey to reawaken your resilience, courage, and strength. Let this book be the catalyst for your transformation, guiding you to shine brightly, unapologetically, and become truly unstoppable.

> "I can be changed by what happens to me. But I refuse to be reduced by it."
>
> *- Maya Angelou.*

Keosha S. Edwards

Hijacked by Shame and Guilt: Reclaiming Perseverance

Keosha S. Edwards

Uncovering the Impact of Shame

I developed a strong passion for helping people overcome shame and guilt due to the pervasive presence of shame and guilt as barriers in many people's lives today. Experiencing shame can have a significant impact on self-esteem. It may contribute to feelings of worthlessness, self-blame, and a negative self-image. This realization dawned on me during a group reading session of a book with a few other women. As we delved into the workbook, the second question hit me like a ton of bricks: "Who are you right now? LIKE REALLY, WHO ARE YOU?" The inquiry encompassed values, expectations, desires, wants, needs, family life, culture, beliefs, and experiences.

Contemplating this question left me stuck, unable to define myself. It was a profound moment when God whispered to me, revealing that I had built so many walls around myself that I had lost my true identity; it had been hijacked by shame. Shame had taken root in me years ago and had been constructing these barriers. In that moment, God conveyed, "I see you; others see you, but YOU don't see you." In that moment, I realized that I simply existed; I couldn't see past the present week. To be honest, I didn't think I mattered. I sat with this realization for about a week, recognizing the need to dismantle these walls.

Reflecting on the past, the Lord showed me a specific time when I had actively built walls to avoid being seen. It was during my pregnancy with my youngest child. I was about five to six months along, and I had already ended the relationship with the father of my two youngest children. I had been in and out of a relationship with him since I was a teenager in middle school. Shockingly, I discovered that two other women were also pregnant by him. I was in disbelief, having just undergone an abortion in an attempt to free myself from the relationship.

Although the decision to terminate the previous pregnancy had been agonizing, I felt compelled to sever ties completely. My heart urged me to keep the baby and walk away from the relationship, but I didn't; I did it my way. The guilt weighed heavily on me after the abortion. Then less than eight weeks later, I found myself pregnant again with my youngest child. What now? I'm pregnant and so are these other women. I dared not think about getting another abortion after all the heartache I had endured. Building the walls and closing everyone out was the route I took. Despite having two baby showers, where people expressed their love for me and my unborn baby girl, the feeling of genuine love seemed elusive. Shame seemed to occupy my thoughts, particularly concerning the father of my child, who attended one of the showers – an event to which he was reluctantly invited. I refrained from inviting him to the second gathering as shame overwhelmed me. I found solace in the absence of his presence among my family.

The Lord asked me, "Where does shame come from?"

After pondering for a few minutes, I responded, "From the opinions of others."

He questioned further, "So why do you care?" He reassured me by saying, "First of all, you didn't get those women pregnant; that is not your problem. Those children are not your responsibility."

The weight of having aborted the previous pregnancy and the worsening situation made me feel remorseful. I cared because I couldn't believe I let this happen to me again. "I truly did not desire to terminate my previous pregnancy." The aftermath had left me burdened with a profound sense of depression, and now I find myself at this juncture. It became imperative for me to cease self-judgment and to confront the mistakes that I made. The question now arose: Where do we proceed from this point? After numerous years of messy cycles, broken promises, and false hope for a situation that was beyond repair, particularly when individuals avoid confronting their brokenness, my childhood wounds remained unaddressed, and only the Lord understands the depths of his struggles. God to dismantle the existing foundation and reconstruct it. This involved letting go of all negativity and self-blame. My perspectives, thought processes, and everything about the way I viewed things had to undergo a thorough evaluation. This was the catalyst for self-improvement and behavior modification. I couldn't be a part of this anymore; it was time to move on.

Renewal and Empowerment

To counter these negative thoughts, I started affirming God's truth about myself and rejecting anything outside of it. I declared that negativity couldn't reside in my mind any longer; it was time for eviction. The Lord consistently reminded me that I am spirit-filled, and since He dwells within me, there's no reason to let shame, rejection or abandonment invade my space. I had to serve them an eviction notice. My story needed to be rewritten, and that's the narrative that must take center stage in my thoughts. It's not always an easy task, but we have to believe we are worth the fight. When we remind ourselves of our values and who we are on this earth, we fight for greatness within us.

Believing in oneself and recognizing one's inherent worth is a powerful and essential aspect of personal development. Self-worth forms the foundation for resilience, determination, and the ability to face challenges with a positive mindset. When we remind ourselves of our values and purpose, we reinforce our commitment to personal growth and well-being.

Life is filled with obstacles and difficulties, but having a strong sense of self-worth can provide the motivation needed to overcome them. It's a journey of self-discovery and self-empowerment. Recognizing the greatness within ourselves means acknowledging our strengths, talents, and unique qualities. Embracing this greatness can fuel our efforts to pursue our goals and make a positive impact on the world.

Moreover, understanding and valuing ourselves can contribute to building healthier relationships with others and ourselves. When we cultivate a positive self-image, we are better equipped to connect with others authentically and contribute positively to our family.

In moments of doubt or challenge, it's crucial to revisit our values, reflect on our accomplishments, and celebrate the progress we've made. This can serve as a source of inspiration and a reminder of the strength within us. It's an ongoing process, but the belief that we are worth the fight is a mindset that can lead to personal fulfillment and a more meaningful life.

While reading a devotion, I came across a powerful statement that read: "Early-life rejection is a significant predictor of shame." It also emphasized that a lack of secure bonding, stemming from unsafe and inconsistent caregiving, contributes to a profound sense of shame (Covenant Counseling Service Being Whole). This statement hit me hard, causing me to pause and reflect.

As a child, the adults, who were responsible for my caregiving, were frequently engaged in alcohol or drug-related activities, with the exception of my mother's mom, in whose hands we often landed. She was a God-fearing woman. This realization of early-life rejection led me to a profound insight, which was that the shame I experienced had deep roots in my childhood. As a child, I often felt as though my needs were not important. I didn't feel as though I was worthy of love and acceptance. There were a lot of closed doors in my environment. I was forced to care for myself at a very young age, which caused me to become very independent and resilient.

My shattered identity, a result of brokenness where emotions, intentions, and perception were in disarray, assumed the worst at times. However, as God gradually reconstructs the fragments of my life, a clearer picture of my true self emerges. No longer scattered, my pieces are laid out, revealing a more cohesive identity in the making. While the process continues, there's a discernible transformation from mere scattered pieces to a more meaningful wholeness.

The Lord emphasizes that resisting negative thoughts and embracing His word and truth strengthens one's belief. Declining access to harmful thoughts leads to empowerment and allows one to internalize and affirm God's truth, which counteracts false beliefs. God has already written our stories, and we have to come into alignment with His story for our lives. Upon reclaiming my identity, I could no longer solely credit and define myself as a great mother to my children because that is the role in which God assured His constant presence in my life. It was time for me to acknowledge the woman that God had created within me. Throughout my life, I've been one to offer uplifting words to those around me. Now, it was time to extend that encouragement to myself.

As a woman who loved to help others, there I stood, giving myself grace and accepting the help I needed to heal. I sought support from therapy and turned to God for guidance. While the Lord can guide me in recognizing some of these issues, seeking therapy was and is essential for learning coping mechanisms and navigating through these challenges.

Commitment to Healing and Wholeness

I've always considered myself to be a strong woman, but going through your healing process challenges your strength. Someone asked the question: "Will you persist in the pursuit of wholeness, or will you succumb to giving up?" Personally, I am committed to continuing the fight for wholeness. Each day, I remind myself that I am fearfully and wonderfully made. I am rewriting my story to reflect blessings, prosperity, victory, health, strength, wisdom, and talent. Shame of no kind can reside here; I have lost so much of myself due to SHAME, as a child and as an adult. I have been picking up the pieces and reclaiming my life. I am a woman of purpose loved by God.

Now, I can answer the question, "Who are you at this very moment? I mean, truly, WHO ARE YOU?" This question rummaged around in my values, expectations, desires, needs, family dynamics, cultural influences, beliefs, and life experiences. I am a woman of intrinsic value, who is destined for greatness and fueled by purpose. My aspirations include being surrounded by genuine love and care from those who truly appreciate me, without the fear of being exploited.

In my journey, I yearn to extend wholehearted love and care to everyone whom I encounter. I seek to express my voice, without fear of vulnerability, and I long for a safe space to share my true self. The desire to be heard and understood is complemented by the need for a secure place where I can openly reveal my vulnerabilities. My deepest longing is to love my family unconditionally and embrace our unique differences. I aspire to respect their individuality and perspectives, while fostering an environment where they feel heard. I am committed to learning about those around me and providing a safe haven for authenticity.

Reflecting on my life, from my early years, I've sensed the whisper of God encouraging me to take on challenges, whether it be riding a bike with a flat tire down a hill or putting on rollerskates and taking those initial steps. His guidance has empowered me to navigate through various experiences and allowed me to accomplish things for which I lacked tangible examples. The voice of God has been a constant source of strength, enabling me to overcome challenges and achieve milestones throughout my life. God gave me the strength and tools to persevere.

P-Persistence: You have to push through even when things get tough.

E-Endurance: You have what it takes to withstand the pressure of life.

R-Resilience: You have the ability to bounce back from challenges.

S-Steadfast: You are unmovable and committed to your path; keep going.

E-Effort: You put your best foot forward; you can do it.

V-Valor: You display exceptional courage and determination, which means you can do this.

E-Excellence: You are outstanding, exceptional, and able to do whatever you put your mind to doing.

R-Result: You get it done; give it your very best.

E-Eager: Eager reflects the positive mindset in YOU, and a proactive approach to life, showcasing a readiness to embrace challenges and opportunities with enthusiasm.

Persevere through the challenges of life. Shame seeks to kill, steal, and destroy the plan of God for our lives. God offers us grace, strength, and forgiveness in the face of adversity. Take control of your narrative; you're the sole author of the story. Those observing from the outside likely have more significant issues than you do. Instead of dwelling on their opinions, remember if God be for you, who can be against you? (Romans 8:31). "And we know that God causes everything to work together for the good of those who love God and are called according to his purpose for them" (Romans 8:28). Let's shift our focus to God's plan for our lives and trust in Him to guide us. Enjoy your journey!

Dr. Candice P. Parker

Breaking Chains: The Journey to Self-Forgiveness and Freedom

Dr. Candice P. Parker

Self-forgiveness is the key that unlocks the chains of guilt, setting our spirits free to embrace the beauty of our humanity and the power of redemption.
– Dr. Candice P. Parker

In the depths of my childhood, forgiveness emerged as a perplexing mystery — a puzzle entwined with conflicting biblical teachings and unspoken words and emotions. Throughout my upbringing, I embraced the belief that forgiveness was a divine act, a pathway granted by God to transcend past mistakes, courtesy of Jesus Christ's sacrifice for our sins — past, present, and future. However, within me, a whirlwind of unresolved emotions — confusion, anger, guilt, and disappointment — swirled, imprisoned within a silence that I couldn't break, and left me to ponder the reasons behind my experiences growing up.

In my adolescence, the conviction that God forgives us regardless of our actions left me feeling confined and struggling to articulate my inner turmoil, which was arising from the actions of others or from those whom I imposed upon myself. Growing up in an era where questioning or challenging authority was viewed as disrespectful, I found myself stifled, lacking an outlet for my lingering questions and emotions.

What was I to do with these internal voices of unanswered questions and buried emotions? Writing about forgiveness transcended being a mere choice; it evolved into a necessity — a compelling call from a journey, seeking emotional healing and a deeper understanding of my inner self. This exploration of forgiveness went beyond unraveling conflicting teachings and personal emotions; it was a quest to bridge the gap between what I was told and what I genuinely felt. It was a voyage toward emotional stability and understanding — a mission delving into the intricate maze of the heart to discover peace and gain a true understanding of the decision and the ongoing journey of forgiveness.

Embarking on the path of forgiveness marked the beginning of a profound journey in my early twenties; the journey began amid the whirlwind of my senior year in college and the arrival of my daughter. The wake-up call was the realization that, to be the mother she deserved, I had to confront the tumultuous mess of untold stories and emotions, also known as my personal Tasmanian Devil. Prior to this, my life was a performance — a facade of good grades and a pretty and tough-girl attitude — all concealing the pain and rejection I carried. However, the outward appearance wasn't enough to evade the reality that I'd been escaping since childhood — the traumas and distorted perspectives on forgiveness.

Fast forward to single motherhood, which was a harsh truth that knocked on my door. At 14, a decision to undergo an abortion left echoes of numbness, anger, and an undeniable chip on my shoulder. For the sake of my daughter, addressing the trauma, seeking spiritual guidance, and confronting the emotional turmoil linked to that significant event became unavoidable. I grappled with the misconception that forgiveness was merely repentance, expecting God to wipe the slate clean. Regardless of how many prayers I offered, the anger, shame, and guilt lingered like an unwelcome guest. Obedience didn't erase the void, revealing that forgiveness isn't just a transaction; it's a complex journey woven into the fabric of my past. Aligning my soul, mind, will, and emotions with what God did when He sent his son, Jesus Christ, to die on the cross became crucial.

My journey through both my professional career and ministry has deeply influenced my personal life, particularly in the realm of healing and navigating the path of self-forgiveness. Reflecting on those years, I am profoundly grateful for how God orchestrated every aspect of my life, placing individuals in my path to aid me in my growth as a woman. As I ventured into helping individuals overcome life's challenges, particularly steering clear of the grip of drugs and alcohol, I held fast to a steadfast motto: "Practice what you preach." It was essential for me not to be the one who offered hope and treatment to others while avoiding facing my own demons when I returned home.

This conviction traces back to my upbringing, where I witnessed a stark contrast between the counsel offered by some of my family members, particularly the women, and their actual behavior. I resolved not to fall into the trap of hypocrisy – doling out advice while simultaneously tolerating unhealthy relationships with men and family members, neglecting to address the pain or trauma from their own childhood, or resorting to verbal, emotional, or physical abuse in response to hurt, lies, or betrayal. Moreover, I was determined not to shield my daughter from witnessing accountability evasion for poor choices or a refusal to apologize for mistakes by feigning ignorance.

While assisting others in their struggles, I confronted my own traumas, notably the journey towards self-forgiveness for deciding to have an abortion at 14. Access to trained therapists, clinical supervisors, biblical counseling, and spiritual advisors played a pivotal role in my forgiveness and healing journey. These resources guided me through the challenges of the first decade of motherhood, unveiling the transformative power of forgiveness.

I've learned that forgiveness is not a one-time act but an ongoing process. It's a deliberate choice to release negative emotions, such as resentment and anger, towards oneself or those who have wronged us. This conscious decision initiates an enduring voyage, freeing oneself from emotional burdens rooted in trauma, betrayal, disappointment, abandonment, or rejection. The essence of forgiveness lies in its role as a continuous journey, actively fostering personal healing and promoting growth.

I confronted the painful memories of shame, guilt, and anger that surrounded my teenage pregnancy and the profound impact of my decision to undergo an abortion on my mental well-being. For six years, I existed in a state of emotional numbness, haunted by flashbacks of lying on the hospital bed as they performed the procedure, and grappling with bouts of anger when I struggled to articulate my emotions effectively.

Granting forgiveness to myself and to those who were directly or indirectly involved in the abortion was a gradual process. Instead of burying myself in work, education, or other distractions to avoid confronting my inner turmoil and the negative self-talk that plagued me with labels like "killer" or "failure," I chose to extend grace to myself. I allowed myself to fully experience and surrender each negative thought and flashback to God. Every time I resisted the urge to flee from the pain and instead embraced the entirety of my truth, I found myself opening up to receive the forgiveness that Jesus sacrificed His life for on the cross.

It was as if I were painstakingly reassembling the shattered fragments of my being, finally allowing myself the opportunity to heal and move forward.

During this journey, I recognized triggers that impacted me, especially during significant milestones in my daughter's life, such as her kindergarten graduations, recitals, school dances, involvement in sporting events, and the anniversary date of the abortion. Each instance stirred feelings of shame and guilt within me, leading me to question my worthiness as a parent. Feeling like an imposter because I didn't keep my first pregnancy, I grappled with the contradiction of loving my daughter immensely and feeling guilty for being present, showing affection (in the form of hugs and kisses to my daughter). I felt ashamed and disgusted when my daughter would run into my arms when I picked her up from school or the after-school programs, and she would smile, give me hugs, kisses and say, "I love you, Mommy!" Inside I was broken, and thoughts plagued me, such as: "If she really knew that I was a murderer, would she still say those things?"

The effects of the abortion weighed heavily on me, hindering my ability to be the best mother and woman that God created me to be. I grappled with the weight of guilt for not having the courage, at 14, to say that I wanted to keep the baby, no matter the disappointment I saw on my mother's face, no matter if I had to give up my aspirations and goals to run track in college. I grappled with the weight of guilt for making that decision, despite the lies told by the individual who impregnated me, despite his accusing me of "being easy" and throwing myself at him, and despite him saying that the child wasn't his. I was accused of trying to ruin his opportunity to go to college and play football, and I endured hardships from my peers at school calling me "a slut", "a baby killer", etc. Additionally, the abortion procedure itself was traumatic, leaving me with haunting memories and unresolved emotions. However, I've come to understand (through healing) that the shame, guilt, and anger stemmed from my past experiences and did not define my ability to love and nurture my daughter.

As a 14-year-old girl, I was unable to articulate my feelings or seek support; I was carrying the burden of shame and guilt alone. Confronting these memories required me to embrace the teachings of Matthew 18:21-22, where forgiveness is emphasized as a continuous process. This verse became my anchor, reminding me that forgiveness is not a one-time event but a journey of grace and reconciliation, both with myself and others who influenced my decisions.

Through introspection and guidance, I've come to realize that forgiveness is multifaceted. It involves acknowledging the pain caused by others and oneself, understanding the context of those actions, and ultimately choosing to let go of resentment and bitterness one memory at a time. It's a process of healing wounds and restoring relationships, both with God and self.

The journey towards self-forgiveness was not easy. It required me to confront deep-seated emotions, reevaluate my beliefs and values, and ultimately choose to extend grace to myself. I had to let go of the notion that I was unworthy of love and forgiveness; I had to recognize that my worth comes from God alone. In embracing forgiveness, I've experienced profound healing and transformation. It has allowed me to break free from the shackles of shame and guilt, enabling me to live a life of purpose and fulfillment. Forgiveness has empowered me to embrace my past, not as a source of shame, but as a testament to God's redemptive power.

Today, I stand as a testimony to the transformative power of forgiveness. I've witnessed firsthand the impact it can have on one's life, freeing them from the bondage of past hurts and enabling them to live in freedom. My journey towards self-forgiveness has taught me invaluable lessons about grace, mercy, and the unconditional love of God.

I learned that forgiveness is a journey that requires courage, vulnerability, and faith. It's a process of letting go of the past and embracing the future with hope and confidence. As I continue on this journey, I am reminded of the words of Jesus, who said, "Forgive us our sins, as we forgive those who sin against us." May we all have the strength and courage to extend forgiveness to ourselves and others, knowing that in doing so, we experience true freedom and healing.

In sharing my personal journey, my aim is to dismantle the misconceptions surrounding forgiveness, paving the way for peace, healing, and reconciliation in your life, thus enabling you to walk in the wholeness that God intended for you. While forgiveness can be a daunting path, especially when we've been deeply hurt, it's crucial to realize that its scope extends beyond forgiving others; it encompasses forgiving ourselves for the wrongs we've committed. Whether it involves causing harm to others, tolerating toxic behaviors, enduring abuse, or remaining in unhealthy relationships, the journey toward self-forgiveness is complex and multifaceted.

Self-forgiveness is not merely a moral reckoning; it's a fundamental cornerstone for personal well-being and growth. Choosing to forgive oneself is a significant step toward emotional liberation, releasing the heavy burdens of guilt and self-blame. This transformative process creates space for healing and fosters the cultivation of positive emotions.

Moreover, self-forgiveness serves as a catalyst for personal development, prompting introspection and offering an opportunity to glean wisdom from past experiences. It becomes a foundation for resilience, empowering individuals to navigate life's trials with greater strength and fortitude. This transformative journey is not solely about absolving oneself but about evolving into a more compassionate and resilient version of oneself.

The impact of self-forgiveness resonates through various aspects of life, profoundly influencing your mental health. It acts as a potent antidote, easing stress, anxiety, and depressive tendencies that may stem from unresolved self-condemnation. By extending grace to ourselves, we initiate a positive feedback loop that contributes to overall emotional well-being.

Furthermore, forgiving myself for having an abortion has had a profound impact on my relationships with others. One of the most significant changes I've noticed is in my self-esteem and confidence. Letting go of the shame and guilt I carried allowed me to show up more authentically in my interactions. It's like I've shed this heavy burden, and now I feel freer to be myself around others.

Moreover, forgiving myself has opened up space for me to be more emotionally available to the people in my life, especially my daughter. Before, I was so consumed by regret and self-blame that I couldn't fully engage with my daughter and standoffish with others. Now, I find myself more present and attentive to my family and friends needs and feelings, which has deepened our connections and brought us closer together.

Another way self-forgiveness has impacted my relationships is by making me more empathetic and compassionate. Going through my own healing journey has made me acutely aware of the struggles others may be facing when providing substance use counseling, life coaching . This newfound empathy has strengthened my bonds with my family and created a more supportive environment where we can lean on each other for support.

Lastly, forgiveness has given me the resilience and maturity to navigate conflicts and disagreements more effectively. Instead of getting defensive or holding onto grudges, I'm better able to approach conflicts with humility and empathy. This has led to healthier communication patterns and stronger relationships overall.

In essence, forgiving myself for having an abortion has not only brought me inner peace but has also enriched my relationships with others, making them deeper, more authentic, and more fulfilling.

It's very important to remember, as we cultivate compassion toward ourselves, our self-perception improves, fostering healthier connections with others. The ability to forgive oneself becomes a cornerstone for cultivating more authentic and empathetic relationships, grounded in a deeper understanding of our shared humanity.

Self-forgiveness is a transformative journey that leads to emotional liberation, personal growth, and improved relationships. By embracing forgiveness for us, we pave the way for healing and wholeness, aligning with the divine intention for our lives. It's a journey that requires courage, introspection, and compassion, but the rewards are profound — a life filled with inner peace, resilience, and authentic connections with others.

At its core, forgiveness is an act of grace and mercy. It involves letting go of the desire for revenge or retribution and, instead, choosing to extend compassion and understanding to oneself and others. This act of forgiveness does not negate or excuse the wrongdoing but rather acknowledges the humanity and inherent worth of all involved.

Forgiveness is not always easy. It requires courage, humility, and a willingness to confront painful emotions. It may involve a process of introspection and self-reflection, as well as a willingness to acknowledge one's own shortcomings and mistakes. However, the rewards of forgiveness are immense. By releasing the burden of resentment and anger, individuals can experience a profound sense of freedom and liberation.

The journey of self-forgiveness is transformative, offering emotional liberation, personal development, and an enhanced sense of well-being. Now, let me share with you an acronym for forgiveness that can serve as a practical guide on your path to becoming whole.

F - Face the Truth: The first step towards self-forgiveness is acknowledging and facing the truth about our actions and their consequences. This honest confrontation is crucial for genuine healing.

O - Open Your Heart: Cultivate an environment of openness within yourself. Allow your heart to embrace the vulnerability that comes with acknowledging mistakes, fostering a space for emotional healing.

R - Reflect and Learn: Self-forgiveness involves a process of reflection. Learn from your experiences, understanding the lessons they bring. This introspection is key to personal growth.

G - Grant Yourself Grace: Extend grace to yourself, recognizing that everyone is a work in progress. Embrace the reality that imperfections are part of the human journey.

I - Initiate Change: Use the insights gained through self-reflection to initiate positive changes in your life. Channel your growth into tangible actions that align with the person you aspire to become.

V - Value Your Worth: Understand and value your inherent worth. Self-forgiveness is not a concession; it's an affirmation of your worthiness of love, understanding, and compassion.

E - Embrace Healing: Allow yourself the gift of healing. Forgiveness is not a one-time event but an ongoing process. Embrace the continual journey towards emotional and spiritual restoration.

Here are some interactive activities, reflection questions, and scriptures to guide you along the path of self-forgiveness, incorporating the acronym, F.O.R.G.I.V.E.:

Interactive Activities:

1. **Journaling Exercise:**
   - Activity: Set aside dedicated time for reflective journaling. Write down your thoughts, emotions, and insights as you engage with each step of the self-forgiveness acronym.
   - Reflection Questions:
     - How did acknowledging and facing the truth about self-forgiveness impact your emotions?
     - In what ways did cultivating openness within yourself create a space for vulnerability and healing?
     - What lessons did you discover through the process of reflection and learning?
     - How can you actively extend grace to yourself as a work in progress?

- Identify specific positive changes you can initiate in your life based on your insights.
- How does understanding and valuing your inherent worth contribute to the self-forgiveness journey?
- What practices can you incorporate to continually embrace healing in your life?

2. **Scripture Meditation:**
   - Activity: Select relevant scriptures that align with each step of the self-forgiveness acronym. Spend time meditating on these scriptures and allowing them to guide your reflections.
   - Reflection Scriptures:
     - **F - Face the Truth:**
       - *Proverbs 28:13 (NIV):* "Whoever conceals their sins does not prosper, but the one who confesses and renounces them finds mercy."
     - **O - Open Your Heart:**
       - *Psalm 51:10 (NIV):* "Create in me a pure heart, O God, and renew a steadfast spirit within me."
     - **R - Reflect and Learn:**
       - *James 1:5 (NIV):* "If any of you lacks wisdom, you should ask God, who gives generously to

all without finding fault, and it will be given to you."

- **G - Grant Yourself Grace:**
  - *Ephesians 2:8-9 (NIV):* "For it is by grace you have been saved, through faith—and this is not from yourselves, it is the gift of God—not by works, so that no one can boast."
- **I - Initiate Change:**
  - *Romans 12:2 (NIV):* "Do not conform to the pattern of this world, but be transformed by the renewing of your mind. Then you will be able to test and approve what God's will is—his good, pleasing and perfect will."
- **V - Value Your Worth:**
  - *Psalm 139:14 (NIV):* "I praise you because I am fearfully and wonderfully made; your works are wonderful, I know that full well."
- **E - Embrace Healing:**
  - *Jeremiah 17:14 (NIV):* "Heal me, LORD, and I will be healed; save me and I will be saved, for you are the one I praise."

Reflection Questions:

1. **Initial Reflection:**

- What emotions arise when you consider the concept of self-forgiveness?
- How has the lack of self-forgiveness impacted your emotional well-being?

2. **Facing the Truth:**
   - What truths about your actions and their consequences have you been avoiding?
   - How can acknowledging and facing these truths contribute to genuine healing?

3. **Open Your Heart:**
   - In what ways can you create an environment of openness within yourself?
   - How does vulnerability contribute to the process of acknowledging mistakes and fostering emotional healing?

4. **Reflect and Learn:**
   - What recent experiences have provided valuable lessons for personal growth?
   - How can intentional reflection on past actions lead to positive changes in your life?

5. **Grant Yourself Grace:**
   - What areas of your life do you find challenging to extend grace to yourself?

- In what ways can recognizing your imperfections as part of the human journey bring about self-forgiveness?

6. **Initiate Change:**
   - Identify specific positive changes you can initiate in your life based on insights gained through self-reflection.
   - How do these changes align with the person you aspire to become?

7. **Value Your Worth:**
   - In what ways can understanding and valuing your inherent worth impact your self-image?
   - How does recognizing your worthiness of love, understanding, and compassion contribute to self-forgiveness?

8. **Embrace Healing:**
   - Reflect on your current practices for embracing healing. What additional steps can you take in this continual journey?
   - How does viewing forgiveness as an ongoing process align with your understanding of emotional and spiritual restoration?

In conclusion, the journey of self-forgiveness is an intricate and transformative journey that goes beyond the surface of absolution. As we navigate the maze of forgiving ourselves, we unearth profound truths about our actions, choices, and their far-reaching consequences. This journey is not confined to a moral reckoning; it serves as a fundamental cornerstone for personal well-being and growth.

By embracing self-forgiveness, we liberate ourselves from the heavy shackles of guilt and self-blame, creating a spacious realm for healing and the cultivation of positive emotions. This process becomes a powerful catalyst for personal growth, encouraging self-reflection and resilience in the face of life's challenges.

The impact of self-forgiveness extends its healing touch to our mental health, alleviating the burdens of stress, anxiety, and depressive tendencies. As we extend grace to ourselves, we initiate a positive feedback loop that contributes to overall emotional well-being.

Furthermore, the embrace of self-forgiveness ripples through our interpersonal relationships, fostering a healthier self-image that forms the bedrock of genuine and empathetic connections with others.

The acronym for "forgive" — Face the Truth, Open Your Heart, Reflect and Learn, Grant Yourself Grace, Initiate Change, Value Your Worth, and Embrace Healing — serves as a practical guide on this journey to becoming whole. Each step sums up a crucial aspect of the process, encouraging us to confront our truth, open ourselves to vulnerability, reflect on lessons, extend grace, initiate positive change, value our worthiness, and continually embrace healing.

As we incorporate these principles into our lives, we embark on a continual journey, not a finite destination. The path of self-forgiveness is dynamic, offering ongoing opportunities for growth, understanding, and personal development.

May this exploration into the realm of self-forgiveness inspire you to face your truth with courage, open your heart to healing, and grant yourself the grace needed for transformative growth. Embrace the ongoing journey of self-forgiveness as a testament to your resilience, your worthiness of love and compassion, and your commitment to becoming the person you aspire to be. May the grace and freedom found in self-forgiveness guide you toward a future filled with emotional liberation and a profound sense of well-being.

Sherita A. Riley

Heartstrings of Healing: A Chronicle of Self-Love and Self-Talk"

Sherita A. Riley

Delving into the realm of self-talk and self-love has been an exhilarating and exhausting journey for me. It has excited me to know that I can help and empower others. I know and understand the design of human behavior and that self-talk often lurks in the shadows; self-talk is an underestimated force shaping our actions. This topic has become a personal favorite, particularly in my work with clients who, unbeknownst to them, dance with the transformative power of their inner dialogue.

It wasn't until recently that the revelation struck me: Self-talk isn't merely a chatter in our minds; it's an intense force intertwining with the very essence of self-love. As I questioned, "Do you truly love yourself, and, if so, under what conditions?" a profound understanding emerged. I realized self-talk was the silent architect of my own life, obstructing my path in ways I hadn't fathomed because self-love did not live within me.

This realization extended beyond my own experiences to the broader human landscape. Our brains, masterful storytellers, weave narratives that, if left unchecked, can shape our reality. It's a fascinating interplay – our thoughts, often devoid of concrete evidence, can become the architects of our beliefs. Validating feelings and thoughts, while crucial, doesn't negate the fact that our thought processes, even when negative, can mold our perceptions.

Recognizing this truth was a game-changer in my life and in my understanding of the intricate workings of the human psyche. It transformed into a captivating chemistry project, where I put on my metaphorical white lab coat and protective glasses. Each revelation became an opportunity to dissect, research, and analyze the powerful strength of self-talk—a force capable of reshaping destinies. This journey has been nothing short of a thrilling expedition into the uncharted territories of our minds, and I am eager to share the profound insights it has unearthed.

Just as self-talk is deemed to be important, so is self-love. Self-love is indeed a crucial aspect of one's identity and overall well-being. It's a journey that evolves throughout life, influenced by various experiences and self-reflection. For me, self-love became a vital component of my journey when I realized its profound impact on how I perceived myself and how I allowed others to treat me.

Self-love, to me, means recognizing and understanding oneself - embracing one's values, worth, and flaws unconditionally. It's about setting boundaries and knowing how I deserve to be treated. Prior to this realization, I believed I possessed self-love, but deep down, I knew I lacked it. This lack of self-love manifested in passive behavior in relationships, a sense of emptiness, and resentment. I often engaged in passive behaviors, such as allowing my significant other to dictate when and how we spent time together and deferring to their choices even when I had preferences of my own. My quality time often went unnoticed, and I settled without continuing to speak up for myself. This passive behavior stemmed from my belief that my own desires were not as important as my significant other's, leading me to suppress my own needs and wants. As a result, it created a sense of emptiness. Over time, I realized I had neglected my needs and desires, resulting in a disconnect from myself. This eventually led to resentment. As the relationship progressed, a lack of self-love and the resulting passive behaviors caused me to resent my significant other, harboring bitterness towards them for not recognizing my needs and unintentionally enabling my passive behavior. Congruently, I resented myself for allowing the lack of self-love to impact my relationship negatively.

Developing self-love requires identifying and accepting one's feelings, which can be daunting, especially amidst heartbreaks. It demands continuous self-accountability, acceptance, and pushing through discomfort. I understood that nurturing self-love meant redirecting energy towards myself rather than solely focusing on others.

Acknowledging my discomfort with certain aspects of myself - my body, my worthiness of good things, my authenticity - highlighted the absence of self-love. I often presented a version of myself that wasn't truly authentic, attracting relationships that weren't positive or healthy. For years, I found myself constantly putting on a façade, pretending to be someone I thought others wanted me to be. I hid my insecurities behind a mask of confidence, afraid to show my vulnerabilities for fear of rejection. In doing so, I attracted relationships that mirrored this lack of authenticity – ones that were superficial and ultimately detrimental to my well-being. I realized that by not embracing my true self, I was unable to attract the positive and healthy connections I truly desired. It wasn't until I confronted my own brokenness and embraced my flaws that I began to attract genuine and fulfilling relationships. Neglecting self-care and prioritizing others over myself further reinforced this realization.

In recognizing these patterns, I came to understand that my self-love wasn't at its fullest potential. However, this acknowledgment served as a starting point for growth and transformation. It has been a journey of learning to love and accept oneself wholeheartedly, with all its imperfections and complexities. Through self-awareness and intentional self-care practices, I aim to cultivate a deeper sense of self-love and fulfillment.

My long and adventurous journey or the quest into the realms of self-love and self-talk commenced at the shattering ending of my third and seemingly final failed relationship. The echoes of abandonment and rejection rang in my heart, leaving me entangled in a web of self-blame and unanswerable questions about my worthiness of love.

As the fragments of my romantic past lay before me, I embarked on a soul-searching journey, starting with a teenage love that refused to blossom into something enduring. With over a decade invested and leading nowhere, I found myself shackled to a cycle of unfulfilled promises and unanswered "whys." The aftermath left me broken, questioning my identity, and drowning in the cold waters of rejection. I knew the significant impact that continuous brokenness would have on my two beautiful daughters. Although it seemed forced and incomplete, I put back together some of the broken pieces - pieces of the broken me. I picked up and moved on, leaving other parts of me behind.

The subsequent relationship mirrored the patterns of the first – a promise of forever, a beautiful ring, and plans for a wedding that never materialized. The celebrations faded into the background, replaced by a prolonged engagement that ultimately crumbled. A beautiful son emerged from the wreckage, but the pieces of my shattered self lay scattered like a thousand puzzle fragments, waiting to be reassembled. I was, yet again, lost and broken. Yet, this time, I was embarrassed and ashamed that nothing came of the proposal.

Shame became ingrained within me, intertwining with my personal narrative. I was hit with shame knowing I was another statistic: a young, black, single mother with two different babies' fathers. It led me to anticipate judgment from others, fostering a belief that I was inherently unworthy of love. This internalized shame was digging deep into my emotions, compelling me to constantly compare myself to others and question how they effortlessly found love while I remained seemingly incapable. Each failed relationship only reinforced my negative self-talk, reinforcing the idea that I was fundamentally flawed and unlovable. This toxic dialogue became the backdrop for my already painted portrait, by which I evaluated my worth, amplifying my feelings of inadequacy and self-pity.

In stark contrast, the concept of self-love appeared distant and unattainable. I struggled to accept my single status, viewing it as a glaring flaw that warranted giving up altogether. It became apparent that this mindset was a barrier to my growth and happiness. Even in moments of strength, anger, or defiance, shame lingered, driving me to withdraw from others, retreating into solitude as if seeking refuge on a desolate mountaintop. This cycle of shame perpetrated a strong and fast-moving stream of negative self-talk, corroding my self-esteem and sabotaging my relationship with myself.

Internalizing the blame, I rewrote my narrative, convincing myself that I wasn't enough – not pretty enough, not fun enough, not anything enough. However, beneath these surface-level wounds lay the roots of a deeper pain, reaching back to my first heartbreak – the abandonment and rejection by my father. He was supposed to love unconditionally, but he left me feeling perpetually second-best; it felt like an echo of rejection, resonating through subsequent relationships.

This realization unraveled a painful truth: I had internalized my father's abandonment, allowing it to mold my self-talk into a relentless stream of self-doubt. For years, I embraced the belief that I was inherently unlovable, creating an internal dialogue that shared the same sentiments of my father's rejection. Unraveling this truth felt like a monumental admission – yes, I carried "daddy issues".

Nearly a year ago, I confronted the harsh reality that self-love was a foreign concept, a casualty of a broken father-daughter bond. I acknowledged, perhaps for the first time aloud, the roots of my internal struggles. The self-talk, the doubts, and the wounds – all traced back to the silent desert of abandonment, where I gasped for emotional nourishment. In this soul-destroying moment, life felt extinguished; Every step was like dragging myself through the mud, a desperate quest for survival in the void. It was a moment when I believed everything was over, and the plain blank canvas of what life should look like stretched endlessly before me, demanding a journey toward self-love and acceptance in the unforgiving territory of my own soul.

I couldn't continue to live life, taking the blame for other individuals' negative behaviors. I became tired of being upset with myself and sad. I became tired of isolating myself as I feared the judgment of the failed relationships. I didn't want to answer questions to which I didn't necessarily have the answers. I, then, knew that the chains of bondage needed to be broken and that steps to self-love and positive self-talk were going to help me with my transformative journey to healing.

The journey of vulnerability surfaced. I knew I needed to speak my truth: the good, the bad, and the ugly. I was ready to remove the mask of fake happiness and the title of "a strong Black woman" because, in reality, a sista' was tired! Vulnerability allowed me to be open, honest, and forthcoming about myself, my struggles, and my relationships. I was no longer defensive and holding everything inside. I provided myself with an invitation to self-acceptance.

I eagerly embraced the invitation to self-acceptance and immediately RSVP'd to be on a transformative journey. In moments of vulnerability, I found the courage to articulate truths from which I had long shied away, even in the silent narrative of my own mind. With raw honesty, I acknowledged the absence of a father figure in my upbringing, a void that had silently shaped my narrative for far too long. I confronted the past relationships, bravely admitting that I clung to them, not out of love's endurance but from the fear of imminent rejection and abandonment. In the spotlight of self-awareness, I faced the mirror and accepted the disorganized/avoidant threads that shaped my attachment style. This revelation unraveled the patterns and intricacies that had influenced my connections with others. I was afraid that there was no one else who would love me. I wasn't confident in myself.

Most powerfully, I looked deep within and embraced my flaws and differences. No longer shying away, I stood in the spotlight of acceptance, seeing each side as part of my unique self. In this act of courage, I began to write a new narrative – one grounded in acceptance, self-love, and the freedom to be authentically me.

During life's challenges and amidst life's ups and downs, moments of transformation often call for courage, moving us from fear into the light of growth. My story is one of those transformative moments, an experience that demanded not only resilience but also a profound act of self-love. The decision to end a relationship that no longer served my well-being was a decision I had never made before. To draw clear lines and put an end to a relationship, as opposed to just allowing it to fizzle out, was terrifying. It was the fear of the unknown and not knowing how I would be treated because of it. Leaving behind the familiarity was nerve-wracking, but I understood that the repetitive patterns would persist without these boundaries. The courage to make that decision became the catalyst for positive change, a transformative leap into the unknown.

It was a struggle and an uncomfortable journey. The days that followed were a storm of emotions, a struggle against the urge to retreat to the chaos to which I had grown accustomed. The discomfort was REAL! The anxiety was REAL! It was constant physical discomfort, a tightening in my chest, a constricted throat, and tingling somatic symptoms. I wanted to end the uncomfortableness by going back, but I resisted. It was an uncomfortable journey while navigating uncharted waters where the only certainty was uncertainty.

Allowing myself the space to grieve the end of my relationships and what I thought was my "forever" was crucial. I didn't rush through the stages of grief. The pain of detachment was unbearable, and the temptation to revert to what I knew was undeniable. Yet, I allowed myself to feel, process, and mourn the end of what I once believed would be a lifelong connection.

In the depths of despair, I found comfort in self-compassion. I reassured myself that the end of the relationship wasn't a failure but a necessary step toward personal growth. My relationship with God deepened during this tumultuous period. I prayed and sang along to my gospel music. Seeking divine guidance, I asked for clarity and understanding, leaning on a higher power to reveal the purpose behind the painful separation. I always asked God to show me signs. He did; I just needed to accept!

Ladies!! The power of wholeness and healing lives deep within you! If you find yourself fighting with self-love and self-talk, recognize that change is possible. I want to emphasize that you can transform your life towards wholeness with strength, courage, and understanding. Whether it takes one attempt or two, or even three attempts, know that it will be a journey, but your destination of self-love is right ahead of you. Here is something to take with you on your journey:

S - Self-affirmation: Acknowledge and celebrate your strengths and positive qualities.

E - Empowerment: Focus on actions and choices that empower you and align with your values.

L - Love and Kindness: Cultivate self-love through acts of kindness and compassion toward yourself.

F - Forgiveness: Let go of resentment and practice forgiveness towards others and yourself.

L - Learning and Growth: Embrace opportunities for personal growth and continuous learning.

O - Operate in Mindfulness: Practice being present in the moment and cultivate awareness of your thoughts and feelings.

V - Visualization: Use positive visualization to imagine and manifest your desired outcomes.

E - Emotional Regulation: Develop skills to manage and regulate your emotions effectively.

Krystal A. Edwards

Embracing the Journey of Self-Discovery: From Limitations to Limitlessness

Krystal A. Edwards

In this season of hills and valleys, I find myself in a state of growth, elevation, and, most of all, transformation. But I need to be transparent. I AM STILL A WORK IN PROGRESS!

I will acknowledge that I'm still becoming familiar with this version of myself, as God's blueprint comes with wide, narrow thresholds and countless left and right turns. I am constantly evolving and discovering new aspects of the Creator, therefore discovering new pieces of myself. The more I discover about my Father in heaven, the more I uncover parts of me that I had been clueless to recognize and acknowledge. This version of me is characterized by reduced self-criticism and a newfound confidence mainly in the higher power that created little ole me, God.

Scratch that; if my God is bigger than anything I could see, think, or imagine, and He lives in me, then I can no longer refer to myself as little. If everything about Jesus, who is God in the flesh, is big, and I identify with Jesus, then I need to identify with His greatness and limitlessness.

Reaching this point was a challenging journey. It required me to deeply explore and understand my identity from a humanistic and spiritual perspective. I had to cultivate emotional resiliency and self-awareness along the way. It was essential for me to embrace the truth that God's creation of me is sufficient to overcome any feelings and experiences of rejection, disappointment, self-doubt, trauma, and failure.

As a therapist, I have had the privilege of working with many individuals who have struggled with their sense of identity. I have observed that many people attribute this lack of self-awareness to their upbringing and the influence of those who raised them, or in some cases, the absence of guidance altogether. Unfortunately, identity is often overlooked or needs more attention while raising children.

Many parents may have needed a clearer understanding of their own identity, which can make it challenging for them to guide their children in discovering their own value and embracing their unique qualities. I can relate to feeling clueless about where my own identity began and what it truly meant from childhood.

Your childhood is a crucial time in your development. It is one of the shortest periods of your life. However, in that short period, you have no other point of reference for who you are publicly other than what the people around you represent. Some of our more difficult challenges occur in that short stage of life. And from those challenges, we start having internal monologues about who we think we are. A lot of what we believe about ourselves, good and bad, started here. During adolescence, we rely on external influences such as family, friends, and society to make decisions, identify who we are, and determine the direction of our lives. It is crucial that children be invited to have a relationship with God as He is the one who began a good work in them, and He is the one who will finish it. Without this relationship, children and emerging adults anchor themselves to lies about who they are and half-truths about who they can become.

It is always possible to embark on a journey of self-discovery and cultivate a strong sense of identity. Through self-reflection, seeking support from trusted individuals, and exploring our interests and passions, we can uncover the beauty and potential within us. It is a lifelong process, but one that is worth pursuing to live a fulfilling and authentic life.

Some people believe that we have a sense of identity when we are born, although it may still need to be fully developed. They also believe that predetermined factors, such as genetics and the shaping influences of our upbringing, personal experiences, and environment, influence our identity.

Others believe we are born as blank slates, waiting for external influences to determine who we will become. However, we are born with a sense of identity that is unique to each individual. I believe God has intricately crafted each of us, placing qualities and characteristics that reflect His image and not his physical appearance within us.

The portrayal of Jesus as a white figure has unfortunately been used to exclude and disqualify individuals from diverse racial backgrounds, like myself. However, it is important to recognize that the concept of being made in God's image, as described in Genesis 1:26-27, and the affirmation that Jesus is the image of the invisible God, as mentioned in Colossians 1:15, go beyond physical appearance.

The reference to the image of God in these passages does not pertain to skin tone or physical beauty. These qualities are not what defines our identity as children of God. As a young black girl, I struggled to reconcile my own identity with the images of a white Jesus that surrounded me. I questioned how I could be made in the image of God when my appearance did not match the depictions I saw.

However, I eventually understood that our physical attributes, such as skin color, do not truly matter. The character, speech, and heart of a person hold the most value. When I embraced this truth, it felt like I had finally made progress in breaking down the barriers that had confined me.

I learned that my identity as a child of God is not determined by my skin color but by my relationship with Him and the qualities I embody. This realization was a significant breakthrough in my journey of self-discovery and acceptance.

Through my journey of self-discovery, I have come to realize that a heavy burden of negative emotions and experiences was suffocating my true identity. The weight of rejection, disappointment, colorism, self-doubt, feelings of worthlessness, trauma, and failure had overshadowed my true self and prevented me from embracing my unique qualities and potential. However, I have learned that these challenges do not define me. They are merely experiences that have shaped me but do not determine my worth or limit my ability to grow and thrive. By acknowledging and processing these emotions, I have been able to release their grip on my identity and rediscover the strength and resilience within me.

Healing Generational Wounds: Confronting the Enemy's Attacks on Identity

On this journey, I've faced many challenges that tested my strength and fortitude, but those challenges pushed me to confront my limiting beliefs and attitudes. However, to confront my attitude and limited beliefs, I also had to develop self-awareness: an awareness of my patterns, habits, negative thinking, and all the heartbreaks, disappointment, doubt, and fears that had played a part in shrinking the big God that lives in me. I had shrunk so much that I even started to suffocate God. Not only was I suffocating God, but I had begun serving other gods, such as anxiety, depression, rejection, resentment, abandonment, anger, and self-hatred. They all ruled over my life, and I served them daily. There were days on this journey when I served them better than I served God.

Here is some more truth I'd like to share with you: I didn't always love the skin that I was in. People had very little appreciation for this little chocolate-skinned black girl, or so I thought. That could be what the enemy wanted me to believe. Believing I was too dark to fit in anywhere. My mother told me that when my great-grandmother met me for the first time as a tender-aged child, her words weren't to let me see my beautiful granddaughter with whom we share the same birthday. Nope, she said, "Why is she so BLACK?" Being this black felt like a curse, and for years, it kept me from serving God and accepting His invitation to His joy and His peace.

This was a generational thing that ran DEEP. This was a generational attack sent by the enemy. My great-grandmother's children would, too, endure this same treatment, which I would learn years later. I often wish I knew her story because I was haunted by an enemy that had hunted her and had set its eyes on destroying a generation of people that I love. Throughout my life, I have learned that the enemy's plan has always been to destroy us from the inside out.

My heart was broken, and I had to identify how it had gotten that way. I had to look at the nasty infection that I had been trying to hide and self-medicate. I had to acknowledge that I had been trying to treat a condition that I hadn't yet examined. I had no idea that the medicine I was using to treat my broken heart wasn't working. I went out and found the biggest bottle of Avoidance 500mg, Anger 1000mg, Isolation 1500mg, and Shame 400mg (because it was my fault for allowing myself to get this sick). My medicine cabinet was full of drugs that did nothing for my condition but made it worse. I found myself addicted to my pain. I'd popped these bottles open daily and prepared to swallow hard without a chaser.

Throughout life, that line you're so black has haunted me. Standing in mirrors, I tried my hardest to scrub away this blackness, and when I couldn't, I made myself invisible. If I couldn't be invisible, then I'd be aggressive. What I wanted was to be left alone. Tar baby, Blacky, ugly, darkness, and if someone were angry with me, that'd call me a black, you know the rest. Here is a truth I rarely share: I didn't want to have a dark-skinned child. I feared she would face some of the same hardships I encountered throughout my childhood. Because while the enemy uses our family, he also uses the other people around us to taunt us, shame us, and guilt us into never feeling like we would be enough. For years, people would make crude jokes about my complexion, and they had no idea the damage it did to my heart, which would result in me seeking acceptance from people who, too, were broken and lost.

At a very young age, I developed the belief that I would never be enough because of the color of my skin. I looked back over my life, and I realized that I purposely sheltered myself to avoid human interaction. If people didn't see me, they wouldn't see how ugly I was. This ugliness turned to anger, rejection, distrust of people, broken relationships, poor partner choices, and chasing after acceptance and validation. There were days when I prayed for God not to wake me up. I started to blame myself for being born this way. I even became my bully. You're not pretty or smart enough; I could go on and on. I hated myself. I hated myself simply because the words catapulted at me most of my life. I went to sleep angry and woke up more furious every day because GOD, why are you still waking me up in a world where I wasn't welcome? I learned that Jesus wasn't welcomed here either, but He never used it as an excuse to give up.

For many years, I carried negative core beliefs about myself that were mirror reflections of the broken people I called family and the broken world around me. But I had no clue that what they projected upon me as a child was a true reflection of themselves. It was their inner monologue that they had been playing on, repeating for most of their lives, and here I was, dancing the same dance to the same song. They were unaware of how broken they were and how they would play a role in feeding our generational curses. For many years, I had no idea how this dance caused me to inflict wounds upon myself that I blamed others for. I had to identify all the things holding me back, including naming myself as the one who was waging war against me. But where did this start? I had to find the root. I had to learn that as children, our natural identities lie in the hands of the people around us, those who pour into us, those who are supposed to nurture us. If the people around you were critical of you, you would likely develop a distorted self-image.

I also understood that my true spiritual identity lies in the invisible God I now joyfully serve. For many years, I was too preoccupied with my natural identity, not realizing I was putting all my efforts into fixing the wrong image. I spent decades adjusting my natural identity to fit the image of man. No wonder I became my bully.

When I discovered I was chasing the wrong god, I decided to give my life to Christ. But after giving my life to Christ, I had to become this new creature. But how? I was broken. I was looking for a quick fix when I gave my life back to Christ as an adult. I wanted Jesus to usher me into my new life. I wanted the reward without doing the work, but that isn't how it works. I wanted healing, and I wanted it now. However, God wasn't going to give it to me until I confronted me.

Like becoming a new creature, I had to work for it day in and day out. I had to resist the devil and the darkness that still lived in me. Yeah, the part where I self-sabotaged because it was easier to dance with failure because that's what I had trained myself to believe.

God wouldn't give me the peace that I desired until I identified that I was my own worst enemy and the devil was my cheerleader. I had to identify all the painful things that happened, and I had to gain an awareness of how I had allowed my pain to dictate my present day. I had to confront my negative thoughts, core beliefs, perceptions, unbelief, and attitudes. I had to dance with the devil and the unhealed version of myself in the wilderness. As an adult, I had to take accountability for what I had control to change. I had to choose whether I would continue to serve my pain or serve my purpose in God.

It required honesty and authenticity. I had to stop reflecting on what others said, did, and believed about me. I had to stop degrading myself and seeing myself as fearfully and wonderfully made. I had to learn to be true to who God created me to be.

This dance with the devil and myself in the wilderness was and still is hard. Sometimes, the Holy Spirit leads me into the wilderness to confront some things that I have not healed from, and the devil always shows up trying to offer me a watered-down version of myself. I have found myself in the wilderness time and time again, and what I've learned about the wilderness is that God is in control of every season that I experience while in the wilderness. I have also learned that the devil is a one-trick pony because every time I find myself in the wilderness, the only thing he can use against me is my past. But I have already lived through those things. I've decided that I would no longer allow the enemy to shame me into reverting to a version of myself that could not speak up for herself, a version of myself that was riddled with anxiety and sadness, the version of myself that would sabotage every good thing that God had prepared for me. In the wilderness, I have learned how to fight the good fight. In the wilderness, I've learned that a butterfly is still a butterfly on its worst day. In the wilderness, I've learned who I am and that my identity started with God and will end with Him as well.

So, girl, tell us what you did. Well, I embarked on a journey of learning how to pivot and understand the delicate art of knowing when to make a move. You see, I had this habit of standing still for the longest time, unaware that God had this intricate blueprint for my life, complete with an Exodus.

I needed to delve into the core of my pain, stare it down, challenge its authority, and boldly declare my freedom from its grasp—no matter its origin. It all began by giving my pain a voice, letting it reverberate through the air. On my quest for self-identity, I faced the persistent ghosts of my past.

The passing of my uncle in 1995 cast a deep shadow, etching an indelible scar on my heart. The longing to strengthen our bond was brutally severed by his tragic murder, a wound that continues to resonate in the depths of my soul. My father's prolonged incarceration, despite his affection for me, introduced a persistent disconnection in our relationship, and its looming presence extended its shadow over many of my subsequent connections with men. As a child, I yearned for male companionship — a consistent father figure and my uncle's presence. I craved connection. However, being my father's sole child proved insufficient to divert him from a life entangled with crime, reinforcing the heartbreaking belief that my presence alone was inadequate.

Addressing the feeling of being an outsider in my family became imperative, as generational curses manifested through criticism rather than love. My mother's battle with depression cast a pall of sadness and loneliness over our home. Financial struggles and moments of darkness amplified the constant sense of insufficiency.

Amidst these challenges, I faced derogatory remarks about my identity — being told I was too black, deemed ugly, forecasted to become a teen mother, and labeled a "tar baby". These words inflicted wounds that lingered. The list goes on, but that is for another book.

Exploring the impact of my pain and embracing its potential for change, I set out on a mission to develop emotional resilience and self-awareness. The goal was to transform the noise of pain into a structured path toward purpose, breaking free from the cycle of dysfunction.

Emotional resilience has been a reliable companion, helping me navigate life's challenges. It enables me to handle difficulties gracefully, replacing negative thoughts with a more positive outlook. As Roy Chowdhury (2019) suggests, emotional resilience is like a symphony that boosts confidence in facing adversity.

Confronting my past, I untangled negative beliefs and crafted a new narrative that revealed my true identity. Self-awareness, akin to a toolkit, exposed the intricacies of my thoughts, emotions, actions, and motivations. This self-awareness extended to recognizing strengths, weaknesses, values, and beliefs — a deliberate process in harmony with my values.

Changing my mindset became a practical goal, a systematic process to reshape my thinking. The introspective process highlighted coping mechanisms as practical tools, effectively managing my emotional responses. Realizing that change requires active participation became evident; it's a gradual, deliberate process.

Motivation played a crucial role, guiding me in taking actions that contributed to a healthier lifestyle. On this journey, pain turned into purpose, dysfunction shifted into harmony, and the intricate dance of emotional resilience and self-awareness created a portrait of resilience, much like a butterfly recognizing its true nature.

In this season of hills and valleys, my heart dances to the rhythm of a profound love for God. I've shaken off the heavy chains of brokenness, discovering a sanctuary within a tribe of kindred souls committed to accountability and healing action. Amidst this journey, I've embraced the truth that my genuine identity lies within, recognizing that the color of my skin has never been a barrier to my connection with God.

Once imprisoned by the notion that unconditional love was beyond reach, I've unraveled those beliefs. Forgiveness has become a kaleidoscope, extending its hues to those who once taunted me, those who departed too soon, and those navigating life without the necessary tools. Yet, most tenderly, forgiveness has graced my own reflection in the mirror.

As you close this chapter and prepare to embark on a new chapter in the book of your life, turning a page in your own story, I challenge you to embrace your inner strength. Confront your feelings of shame, guilt, fear, doubt, and past traumas; honor your resilience. Trust in the beauty of your healing journey and believe in your self-worth and capabilities. Know that you are deserving of love.

Healing is a courageous path, and each step towards healing is a step towards empowerment and self-discovery. You are a beacon of light, a symbol of grace, and a testament to your inner strength. Move forward with courage and compassion as your journey reveals your unwavering spirit and resilience. Now, let me introduce you to an acronym for identity that can serve as a practical guide on your journey to wholeness:

I - Individuality: Embrace and celebrate your unique traits, qualities, and characteristics that make you who you are.

D - Discover: Take the time to explore and discover more about yourself, your values, beliefs, passions, and aspirations.

E - Embrace: Accept and embrace all aspects of yourself, including your strengths, weaknesses, successes, and challenges.

N - Nurture: Care for and nurture your well-being, growth, and personal development to reach your full potential.

T - Trust: Trust yourself, your abilities, and Jesus to help you navigate the hills and valleys of life.

I - Integrity: Live with integrity by staying true to your values, principles, and morals in all aspects of your life.

T - Transformation: Embrace the process of growth and transformation, allowing yourself to evolve and become the best version of yourself.

Y - You: Remember that your identity is unique, and you can shape your identity and create a life that reflects your true self.

In closing, I will leave you with this poem written by my 12-year-old daughter, who sees me and whose love has helped heal me. Let this poem be a reminder that no one in this world goes unnoticed. God sees you, and God loves you in the skin you're in.

"The Skin She's In"

Beautiful little dark-skin girl from the depths of Jamaica.
Trying to fit in without being a faker.
She is hated on for her skin;
why don't they appreciate what she's in?
She tries to speak, but the words linger on her tongue;
she doesn't know where she should begin.

A Beautiful little dark-skin girl
in our cold, cruel world
hating on HER own skin!
Her thoughts swirled
like her beautiful Caribbean curls.
Why doesn't she love the skin she's in?
A beautiful little dark-skin girl, beautiful as can be!
The world must be blinded if they cannot see!
She shines like her name, Krystal,
but she is still stuck in the middle;
she stays silent as she is belittled.
Little dark skin girl called out her name,

just for her skin, she is put to shame?
She deserves much more than the world provides,
so why is her black pride so denied?
Her journey is both light and dark.
Sparked by Jesus, she has gotten a new start.

Now a beautiful dark skin woman, her eyes open,
she is no longer soft-spoken;
she releases the pain she once felt inside;
her old hate flows away like the ocean tide.
She looks at her beauty, and she sees God within!
She is in love with the beautiful skin she's in!
She is free from the chains gripping at her and
free from the haters picking at her!
She is free from degrading
and from haters hating;
she is who she is, and she loves the skin she is in.

Shameka L. Jones

Awakening The Inner Self:
The Healing Power of Mindfulness

Shameka L. Jones

Mindfulness served as a pivotal bridge, aiding in cultivating self-awareness, healing from past traumas, overcoming self-imposed limitations, correcting distorted perceptions, and playing a critical role in my journey to wholeness. If I encapsulate mindfulness into a single term, it would be "awareness."

This practice enables a multifaceted understanding of oneself, revealing one's physical, mental, emotional, and spiritual states. The American Psychological Association (2024) beautifully captures the essence of mindfulness, defining it as "awareness of one's internal states and surroundings. Mindfulness aids in circumventing destructive or automatic behaviors and responses by teaching individuals to observe their thoughts, emotions, and present-moment experiences without judgment or reaction."

Mindfulness is traditionally rooted in Buddhist meditation practices; however, mindfulness also resonates throughout the Holy Bible in teachings that reflect its principles. For example:

- Psalm 46:10 advises believers to "Be still, and know that I am God," promoting a pause for calmness and acknowledgment of God's omnipresence, a concept at the heart of mindfulness.

- In Matthew 6:28-29, Jesus encourages contemplation of the lilies, highlighting effortless growth and advocating for trust in the divine provision, mirroring the mindfulness ethos of living in the moment and releasing anxiety.

- Galatians 5:22-23 lists the fruits of the Spirit, including love, joy, peace, and self-control, which necessitate a mindful reflection on one's thoughts, deeds, and attitudes.

While "mindfulness" is not directly mentioned in the Bible, the underlying principles of being present, conscious, and deliberate in one's thoughts and actions, emphasizing spiritual truths, align closely with biblical messages. Mindfulness is a valuable tool for managing thoughts, emotions, and responses in a healthier, more balanced manner. It is an approach that enhances mental, emotional, and physical well-being, transcending mere practice to become a way of life.

I am eager to share this transformative lifestyle that has made me a better individual — being more self-aware, purposeful, and compassionate, even towards those who have caused me pain. Mindfulness has been instrumental in renewing my mind and facilitating a transformation that I doubt would have been possible otherwise. I aim to spread the word about this practice to anyone willing to listen. I am confident that it can enrich people's lives, whether on a healing journey or simply navigating daily life while fostering continual growth and profound gratitude.

Life Without Mindfulness

Reflecting on my path, I've come to cherish the wisdom and personal growth that mindfulness has gifted me. Before, my life seemed engulfed in dysfunction, deeply marked by past wounds, such as emotional abuse, rejection, abandonment, and shame. These deep-seated wounds stretched their shadows over my life, breeding distrust, a protective stance, and a pattern of sidelining my needs in pursuing others' approval. The fear of rejection was so intense that it compelled me to prioritize the desires of others over my own consistently. Even though God generously filled my cup to overflowing, I kept pouring myself into others' cups until I was empty, neglecting my needs. I acknowledge that my trust issues are an ongoing challenge, affecting my willingness to seek help and, previously, obstructing my ability to form new friendships beyond those of my childhood. It also led me to cling to old wounds.

This baggage made it difficult to repair damaged relationships and open myself up to trust more quickly.

Despite the turmoil boiling inside me, I appeared composed, serene, and well-organized on the surface. No one could have imagined the internal struggle I faced. Externally, I portrayed a picture of control, mastering the art of showing perfection and confidence. Driven by perfectionism, I prided myself on keeping everything under control, a tactic that offered me a feeling of safety. This control extended to my emotions, ensuring I never acted in a way I would later regret, a silver lining to my inclination towards pleasing others. Yet, internally, I wrestled with unexpressed emotions and the weight of past traumas, viewing life through a lens tinted by pain, brokenness, and vulnerability. My faith was like a strong glue holding me together, giving me the inner strength I needed to face what was coming. It kept me from falling apart, and during the tough times, it was like a lifeline, keeping me from losing hope. However, my need to always be in control sometimes stopped me from fully accepting that divine help.

Struggling to let go and trust God's plan, especially when hurt by those I cared about, made it hard for me to trust fully. I also battled with feeling unworthy, not good enough, and loaded down with shame and guilt because of what others thought and my regrets. Feeling ashamed about becoming a mom as a teenager made it even harder to accept God's help. However, my stubbornness and the drive to prove everyone wrong pushed me to change my story and fight against the negative labels from my past. This journey of overcoming shame and defiance against the labels is chronicled in the book I co-wrote, *The Unchained Goddess*, where I delve into the empowering process of facing shame and fostering resilience.

If it were not Shame that would show up, Rejection would haunt me and confirm that I was not worthy or good enough. It got to the point that if I did not get a job I applied for, that rejection would show up and make me feel inadequate, not worthy, and not valuable all over again. People often marveled at my capabilities, questioning how I accomplished so much or praising my proficiency, frequently labeling me perfect. Despite identifying as a perfectionist, I felt far from ideal. Compliments and positive feedback would often go unnoticed by me. There is a saying, "Broken people hear differently," which I found profoundly accurate. In my vulnerability, I uniquely processed words, intentions, and emotions. Even when praised, I could not accept it as truth, continually striving for better, driven by a belief that I was never sufficient. This perspective, which I consider a divine intervention, transformed my negative experiences into positive outcomes. My pursuit of perfection led me to excel and surpass expectations, though it also resulted in exhaustion as I pushed myself to the limit (a habit I'm still trying to amend).

Over time, my mental, emotional, and spiritual health was deeply affected, leading to a decline in my physical well-being. This self-neglect resulted in a gradual increase in weight as I resorted to emotional eating for comfort, often choosing carbohydrate-rich comfort foods during challenging times. Food has always been a significant part of my life, a passion that began in my younger years. Now, it became clear that my connection with food was not merely about pleasure; it was tied to my emotions. Previously, an active lifestyle of running track, playing double dutch, and being constantly on the move helped counterbalance my overeating. However, after the birth of my son and a decrease in physical activity, I began to gain weight, falling into a cycle of weight loss and weight gain throughout my adulthood.

The shadows of my past loomed large, hiding my true potential and, at times, making me invisible —a state I unknowingly accepted amidst deep-seated shame. A sense of rejection and not feeling good enough seeped into my self-perception, undermining my self-assurance. This internal conflict turned me into a chronic procrastinator, held back by a fear of failure and feelings of inadequacy, even as I achieved significant milestones academically and professionally, including obtaining a master's degree. Consequently, this persistent sense of not measuring up became a self-fulfilling prophecy, subtly affecting how I acted and interacted with others. Without realizing it, I projected uncertainty about my abilities, which made others doubt my competence despite my dependability and hard work. This uncertainty often led me to being overlooked. I was passed over for positions and projects well within my capabilities, perpetuating the cycle of self-doubt and undervaluation.

Mindfulness in Action

Upon completing my master's degree, I was in a relentless cycle of job applications, met with rejection at every turn. Throughout my academic journey, I accumulated an additional forty pounds, leading to a profound disappointment in myself despite achieving an educational milestone that once seemed beyond my reach. In this period of struggle, I leaned heavily on my faith, pouring my heart out to God in my prayer journal — a practice I have maintained since childhood, where writing prayers became a source of solace and reflection. Faced with the daunting realities of over $100,000 in student loan debt, weight challenges, and dwindling hope, I earnestly sought divine intervention in 2017, praying for holistic healing across all facets of my life: physical, mental, emotional, spiritual, and financial.

This introspection and plea for guidance led me to a transformative encounter with God, leading me to Romans 12:2, which says, *"Do not conform to the pattern of this world but be transformed by the renewing of your mind."* This scripture encouraged me to embark on a mental and spiritual renewal journey, with self-awareness as its cornerstone. I began to be more aware of my thoughts and behaviors. My exploration led me to discover mindfulness, starting with guided meditations. These practices, focusing on being in the present moment and my immediate experiences, thoughts, and sensations, became crucial for increasing my awareness of my emotions and physical state. Over time, I learned to engage in mindfulness without guidance, realizing that the principles could be applied beyond meditation to every moment of life. This approach allowed me to appreciate the beauty of the world around me and recognize my thought patterns without judgment.

Mindfulness introduced me to a new perspective on nature, self-acceptance, and resilience in the face of disappointment. It gave me the tools to address feelings of rejection, shame, and past traumas. This journey led me to embrace a concept I call "360 Health", which represents a comprehensive approach to well-being, encompassing physical, mental, emotional, social, and spiritual health. It also signifies a return to a state of healthiness, free from the impacts of rejection, shame, and trauma.

Revisiting Romans 12:2, mindfulness embodies the scripture's call for transformation through the renewal of the mind. It fosters a deepened awareness of our thoughts, emotions, and sensations, enabling us to break free from automatic responses and align our lives more closely with our spiritual values. This transformation is a testament to the power of changing our thought processes to improve our overall well-being.

Suddenly, everything clicked. I understood the profound meaning behind Romans 12:2, recognizing that the renewal of my mind was vital in transforming the various aspects of health for which I had been praying. I discovered the critical role of mindfulness in boosting my self-awareness. Unknowingly, I had been applying principles of cognitive behavioral therapy (CBT) even before I was consciously aware of it. My exploration led me to take a CBT course, where I learned that psychological challenges often stem from harmful thought patterns and deep-seated behaviors that are detrimental. My experience with CBT taught me to become more mindful of my thoughts and beliefs and how they impacted my emotions and actions. I learned to identify and confront these negative thoughts, changing my inner narrative to one that is more positive and empowering.

This passage from 2 Corinthians 10:4-5 in the New International Version offers a powerful perspective on spiritual warfare:

> *"The weapons we fight with are not the weapons of the world. On the contrary, they have the divine power to demolish strongholds. 5 We demolish arguments and every pretension that sets itself up against the knowledge of God, and we take captive every thought to make it obedient to Christ."*

In observing thoughts and feelings without judgment, mindfulness aligns with Paul's directive to "take every thought captive to obey Christ." Through mindfulness, I could observe my thoughts, discern the falsehoods within them, and let them go. This process enabled me to dismantle the negative thought patterns or "strongholds" that contradicted God's truths about me. For example, replacing thoughts of inadequacy with affirmations like "I am fearfully and wonderfully made" from Psalm 139:14, or in moments of feeling insufficient, declaring "I am more than a conqueror in Christ" Romans 8:37. Beyond transforming my thought patterns, the most significant impact of mindfulness was entering a state of stillness where I could quiet my mind enough to hear God's gentle voice, guiding and directing me toward healing. In healing, I was able to start my journey of wholeness.

Empowerment and Healing through Mindfulness

My growing self-awareness led to a deeper understanding of myself, enabling me to identify and replace negative thought patterns with positive affirmations. Engaging with uplifting literature and sermons played a significant role in my journey. Yet, mindfulness honestly acted as the key, allowing me to absorb and apply the wisdom I gained fully. This practice guided me toward decisions resonating with my faith, values, and objectives.

Gradually, my confidence emerged, revealing strengths previously obscured by my pessimism. I embarked on a journey of self-discovery, uncovering aspects of myself that were either forgotten or entirely new to me. I learned to love myself in a new light, recognize my value, embrace my imperfections, and shed the false beliefs of being unworthy or insufficient.

Mindfulness enabled me to forgive, marking a significant turning point in my transformation. It fostered a sense of compassion and empathy towards those who had caused me pain in the past, which was essential for genuine forgiveness. By providing a space to process my pain and consider the perspectives of others, I was able to let go of deep-seated bitterness and resentment and, importantly, forgive myself, paving the way for healing and personal growth.

I remember the moment I genuinely forgave my mother; it was unforgettable. Although I thought I had moved past my resentment toward her, I discovered that remnants of childhood grievances lingered within me. Suddenly, a profound sense of compassion washed over me, shifting my focus from her actions to the possible hardships and suffering she experienced. I reflected on her task as a single parent — managing six children by age twenty-five, including two sets of twins — and the overwhelming pressure she must have felt. Then, I felt a surge of unconditional love for her, inspired by a sense of divine grace that seemed to sweep away all the bitterness and resentment. In that instant, I forgave her truly and wholly, letting go of all the pain that had held me back.

This experience underscored how mindfulness and forgiveness naturally lead to compassion. Adopting a mindful approach allowed me not only to acknowledge my suffering but also to extend empathy towards my mother. Mindfulness enhances the ability to empathize with the experiences of others, cultivating a compassionate mindsct.

Cultivating Mindfulness and Renewing My Mind Through Gardening

Starting my gardening adventure in 2021 was a turning point in my journey toward complete healing, profoundly enhancing my mindfulness practice. The words from John 14:27, *"Peace I leave with you; my peace I give you. I do not give to you as the world gives. Do not let your hearts be troubled and do not be afraid,"* powerfully resonated with me as I was planting seeds in my garden. This moment of peace contrasted sharply with the inner chaos fueled by persistent negative thinking. In the tranquility of my garden, I found myself reconnecting with that divine peace, feeling a deep connection with nature and sensing God's presence as tangibly as if He were right there beside me.

A particularly enlightening experience came as I wrestled with a tenacious weed, its roots stubbornly anchored in the soil. I grasped a divine lesson on rooting out long-established weeds in that struggle. This revelation served as a metaphor for the internal "weeds" seeded by past injuries and traumas, which cultivated harmful emotions and thoughts within me. Understanding that healing requires addressing these deep-seated issues, I realized that akin to neglected weeds choking the life from plants, unexamined emotional weeds can impede our journey toward realizing our full potential and purpose.

Gardening also imparted the virtues of patience and acceptance. The realization that plants flower in their own time taught me to embrace life's natural pace, aiding me in overcoming my need for control. This synthesis of gardening and mindfulness cultivated a practice rooted in patience, acceptance, and surrendering control, a lesson I continue to refine.

This fusion of mindfulness with gardening has catalyzed my evolution into an enhanced version of myself. Striving to dwell on the moment, I now greet my positive and negative thoughts without judgment, releasing them and pivoting towards positivity. Daily, I embody the essence of Romans 12:2, allowing the tranquil wisdom of the garden to guide the transformation and renewal of my mind.

Integrating mindfulness into every facet of your journey is imperative as you navigate your path to healing and wholeness. Embrace it, letting its principles of focused attention, non-judgment, acceptance, resilience, and compassion shape your mindset. Mindfulness can be summarized by the acronym A.W.A.R.E.:

- **A - Attention:** Directing attention to the present by observing thoughts, emotions, and sensations as they emerge.
- **W - Without Judgment:** Encountering each moment without categorizing experiences as good or bad but merely acknowledging their presence.
- **A - Acceptance & Awareness:** Welcoming life's experiences without resistance, fostering a state of non-reactivity, and maintaining an acute awareness of one's mental and physical states.
- **R - Resilience:** Build emotional resilience by staying present and engaged, even amid adversity, and facilitating personal growth and learning.
- **E - Empathy:** Cultivating understanding and empathy for oneself and others, recognizing the commonality of human experiences.

Adopting mindfulness becomes essential to self-awareness, laying the groundwork for meaningful healing and significant change. It sheds light on the journey toward becoming your true self, underlining the critical importance of mindfulness in fostering the self-exploration and development that resonates with your inherent potential. Mindfulness has been instrumental in my journey towards healing, forgiveness, building new relationships, and achieving a weight loss of over 50 pounds and counting. It has supported my growth physically, mentally, emotionally, spiritually, and socially. Through mindfulness, I've encountered aspects of myself that were previously unknown. I am continuously evolving and learning to appreciate my being more deeply. Mindfulness is the legacy I aim to pass down to my descendants, guiding them to craft the lives they were divinely designed to lead.

Dr. Janell Jones

Thriving Through Tears: A Guide to Overcoming Grief

Dr. Janell Jones

Navigating through grief is a topic that resonates deeply with me. Before I share my personal experiences, let's unravel the essence of grief. Grief isn't just about the emotions that are tied to loss; it's a complex, everyday part of being human. Loss, in this context, goes beyond death and covers a range of departures and finalities, from the tangible to the intangible. It's in those subtle cracks in life's fabric when relationships, trust, or connections are severed.

This is where my passion ignites in observing how some aspects of life, which are often overlooked, carry the weight of grief. I describe grief as the unraveling of ties or as a severance between a person and something or someone. This can span across diverse arenas — relationships, businesses, friendships, jobs, or any significant life encounter. I believe that we often fail to recognize certain experiences as grief. Consequently, the lack of acknowledgment hinders the proper processing of these emotions, ultimately manifesting as both physical and mental ailments.

My grief journey is marked by two heart-wrenching stories that resonate deeply within me; these are stories that I discussed in my TEDx Talk. The first story is composed of the fading memories of my four-year-old self in the tragic murder of my 17-year-old sister, which was a loss that overshadowed the joy I had of winning a mirror at the State Fair. The second narrative unfolds in a chilling altercation between my father and grandfather, culminating in a shooting and my father's untimely death. These threads of sorrow, woven into the very fabric of who I am, shape my emotional connection with grief. The yearning for a father and the unfulfilled potential of my sister's life are tender highlights in my emotional TEDx Talk on the exploration of loss.

Rick

Not many know about the string of losses that followed, an unyielding current of grief that engulfed my life. When my sister and father died in 1983, I thought I knew grief pretty well, but life had other plans; the hits just kept coming. At only 23, still reeling from one loss, I got word that my big brother, Rick, had cancer: terminal cancer. This was the brother who hated hospitals and who had stared down death in the form of an infection two years before. My brother had beat that ruthless infection through sheer grit but not this time; cancer didn't fight fairly.

That Thanksgiving, he wouldn't leave his room and complained of stomach pain. The truth stared back, cold and hard, even as I tried convincing myself that this was just another scare. My sister's ex-boyfriend begged my brother to get help and somehow got through to him where the rest of us failed. However, nothing could soften the blow of hearing that vicious C-word at the hospital. His cancer had metastasized so far that not even chemo could catch up to it. The doctors gave him weeks, a month at best, to live. I clung desperately to the memory of my miracle brother who had cheated death before. I was certain that he had another comeback roaring inside. Unfortunately, this time, hope slipped through my fingers as I watched cancer consume him pound by pound. In less than a month, his fight ended as he stared into the sky and took his last breath.

Eddie

Back in college, Sundays were catch-up on homework days. - I could be found with my nose crammed in books, trying to power through stacks of assignments. Therefore, when my other brother, Eddie, called on that mundane afternoon, proudly rambling about cooking our mother's dinner (neckbones and potatoes, to be exact), impatience crept in as I half-listened because I was itching to return my focus to my homework. Twenty minutes later, my mom called me, her voice piercing through the phone. She was intoxicated; she and my brother were intoxicated. "JANELLLLLLLL," she said with a mix of nervousness and authority in her tone.

Panic gripped me; I thought I was in trouble. "Yes, mom?"

"Eddie is over here breathing hard, and his eyes are rolling in the back of his head."

My first thought was: Why is she calling me instead of 9-1-1? "WHAT?" I yelled. "Did you call 9-1-1?"

"JANELLLLL," she screamed again.

Without hesitation, I hung up, dialed 9-1-1, and raced to my mom's house, which was just 12 minutes away. In my mind, I prayed that they were performing CPR and saving him. "Please, Lord, not another one of her children gone."

Pulling up to her apartment complex, I saw the firetruck outside. My sister Tina's son, who is my oldest nephew, happened to be passing by, and I flagged him down. I told him that Mom had frantically called me about Eddie's condition. We rushed into my mother's apartment and found Eddie on the floor, lifeless. The paramedics had been tirelessly performing CPR for the entire time that they were there. I raced over, but they couldn't revive him. Desperation gripped me, and I pleaded with them to take him to the hospital. The paramedic gently informed me that he was gone and that even if they took him to the ER, it would cost $500-$1200; there was nothing more they could do. If I had known when he called me earlier that day that it was going to be the last time I'd hear his voice, I would've soaked up every word.

Reece

My ex-husband, Reece and I shared a history that reflected the lyrics of "Fantasy" by Mariah Carey and Ol' Dirty Bastard, taking us back to the innocence of childhood. We grew up as neighbors, and the details of our first meeting are hazy in my memory, honestly. However, the threads of our connection were woven before the age of four, as I recall his grandmother visiting our home to offer condolences after my sister's tragic death.

Our love story unfolded like a classic teenage romance. I found myself pregnant at 16, welcoming our first child at 17. We navigated the tumultuous dance of breaking up and reconciling. After our initial separation at 16, we found our way back to each other at 18. By the time I turned 20, we were married, and two more children enriched our lives. Despite our eventual divorce, we maintained an amicable understanding.

We divorced four years later, and unexpectedly, we plunged into a nightmarish legal battle that spanned nearly a year. In April of that same year, he reached out with an apology, perhaps a glimmer of reconciliation to become co-parents. However, the unexpected turn of events unfolded in July when his sister began calling me at 3:00 AM. The strained nature of our relationship left me puzzled about the urgency of her seeking to contact me, which prompted a game of "phone tag". Anxiety and speculation mounted as I scoured the Internet for information about him possibly being arrested or in trouble.

Checking the news and court records yielded no answers, and I wondered why she would call if he had been arrested.

Finally connecting with her, the gravity of the situation became evident. She was in tears, struggling to articulate the tragedy. Before she could share more, another voice joined the call. It was a cousin, and her words landed like a devastating blow: "Reece is dead." The shock paralyzed me. Despite the custody disputes and lingering resentments, the news hit me harder than expected. As the tears flowed, the reality of the sudden loss left me grappling with the daunting task of breaking the news to our three children, who would be left to mourn the man who was once a significant part of their lives.

Wait, the relentless parade of tragedy wasn't finished with me.

Tina

At this point, I felt as though I had become numb to the sting of death, yet a lingering fear persisted, an apprehension of witnessing its cold touch once more. The procession of loss continued, claiming more family members — first my nephew, then my half-brother, followed by my niece. It was an overwhelming cascade, but nothing could have prepared me for what awaited in the shadows of the next chapter.

Allow me to set the scene. I was the youngest among my mother's six children, a brood of children scattered across time. The age gaps were substantial, with my three older siblings being 26, 25, and 21 years my seniors. My connection with my sister, Tina, ran deep. With Tina acting more as a mother figure due to her 21-year seniority over me, our bond transcended typical sisterhood. Then, in July 2019, the script of our lives took a dark turn Tina had a cough that was believed to be bronchitis, but her persistent cough, which was diagnosed as pneumonia, raised alarms. Antibiotics brought no relief, and concerned, I insisted she visit the ER. In an odd twist, she had already left the ER, which was what prompted my intervention. Rushing her back to the ER, I hoped for the best as she awaited treatment. The call about them wrapping up brought fleeting relief; I was hoping that it wasn't severe. Being familiar with ER protocol, I told her to call me upon discharge. Living just eight minutes away, I awaited the call, bracing for the next chapter in this heart-wrenching saga.

The call reflected a heaviness that gripped my heart. Tina's voice, on the other end, revealed that she wasn't coming home; she was being admitted to the hospital. The air hung heavily with a sense of anxiety, a silent acknowledgment that something was gravely wrong. Subsequently, Tina was admitted to the hospital where I worked. During rounds, where the entire interdisciplinary team convened, I ended up on the same floor, where my sister was admitted, and that wasn't my usual place to be. The doctor's words hit hard: "It doesn't look good." My heart sank. The biopsy was pending, but the imagery revealed a daunting mass in her lungs.

At 61, a chilling diagnosis of stage-three lung cancer unfolded. Denial gripped her; she dismissed the "cancer" label, dubbing it "this thing". She felt overwhelmed as if she was sinking under the heavy burden of her problems. It was an all too familiar feeling of being pulled down into darkness. She withdrew from the world, shunning company and dodging calls. She couldn't come to terms with the cancer, the unwelcome intruder.

The revelation of her diagnosis cast a pall over her life, a shroud of disbelief that she couldn't shake. In an attempt to infuse some semblance of normalcy, we orchestrated a birthday celebration, all while concealing the truth of the cancer diagnosis from our mother, as we were unsure of how she would react. We gathered for the dinner in the absence of the guest of honor. At that moment, we stood at the precipice of a harsh reality, grappling with the unspoken anguish that hung thick in the air.

As time relentlessly pressed on, my sister fought her battle in the quiet recesses of isolation. Despite her yearning for life, the looming specter of impending death clung to her thoughts like shadows. September marked a foreboding revelation; stage 4 cancer had advanced into her brain. To stand by her side, I partnered with my sister's daughter-in-law, sharing the responsibility of taking her to cancer treatments. The painful spectacle of her gradual decline unfolded; it was a heart-wrenching testament to fighting the disease. Trapped in her fears, my sister chose silence over sharing; her deterioration was evident as she stopped eating and drinking. A soul-stirring moment imprinted itself in my mind when she confided in me that she was hearing voices and became infused with hope through a dream. In the vision, she was healthy and vibrant, and she assured me that everything would be okay. In my hopefulness, I misinterpreted it as a sign of triumph over cancer. Little did I know that it was a foreboding preview of the impending farewell. This agonizing dance with grief before the final act was the cruel prelude to loss. It is what they call "anticipatory grief".

Anticipatory grief, as defined by Forbes, is "the anguish one experiences in the days, months, or even years leading up to the death of a loved one or another impending loss". In my sister's case, as much as we tried to shield ourselves from the harsh reality, the hard truth lingered; we knew she was slipping away. Her once-vibrant body withered before our eyes as she was tethered to the hospital for chemotherapy and to battle dehydration. A mere 78 pounds bore the weight of her diminishing vitality.

Anticipatory grief doesn't diminish the depth of sorrow that one feels upon the loss; rather, it signifies a peculiar form of readiness for the inevitable. This nuanced experience stands in stark contrast to the abrupt and unforeseen grief that can strike with a ferocity of its own. On November 29, 2019, my sister lost her battle with cancer. Adding to the sorrow, her husband had passed away the Monday before she did, leading to a heart-wrenching joint funeral that highlighted the interconnected web of grief in our lives.

Mommy

Putting myself in my mother's shoes felt like an impossible task. At 86, she had already endured the heartbreaking loss of four children, each one marking a somber burial. Her resilience stood as a testament to the strength inscribed by life's relentless storms. However, in 2020, a year marked by the tumultuous grip of Covid, unexpected challenges lay ahead. The fear of the unknown cast a looming shadow as the pandemic unfolded globally, claiming countless lives. What initially felt distant, as it related to the COVID-19 pandemic, gradually encroached upon our lives.

In October 2020, my mother's world took a painful turn when she fell at her apartment. Swiftly carried to the hospital by ambulance, her fractured leg revealed the need for recovery in a skilled nursing facility. Reluctant to step into another facility and fearing the potential of contracting COVID-19, she chose the alternative, which was to return home with me. Assigned both physical and speech therapy to aid her healing, my mother made commendable progress. Only a week away from returning to her apartment, a sudden twist of fate unfolded. During a routine visit to therapy, her physical therapist detected a fever and abruptly ended the session. Urged to seek Covid testing, we rushed to the local hospital. Within 24 hours, the diagnosis was confirmed; it was Covid-19. In consultation with her physician, I learned that if her oxygen levels dipped below 88, returning to the hospital was imperative.

Confronting the harsh reality, I checked Mom's oxygen levels — 86 on the pulse oximeter. With a heartfelt plea, I insisted, "Mom, we need to go to the hospital."

She staunchly refused, claiming, "I'm okay." In that moment, the looming battle against Covid became a clear, stark reminder of life's fragility.

We headed to the hospital, where I wheeled her into the emergency room. I was aware that if she had COVID-19, I likely did, too, so I kept my distance and was unable to accompany her. Little did I know, it marked the last time that I'd see Mom coherent. Her two-week struggle against Covid unfolded in the hospital, bringing sleepless nights that were filled with worry and a loss of appetite. The MyChart app became my constant companion in my desperate search for positive updates. Urgent calls from the doctors on December 8th prompted my sister and me to go to the hospital, where we faced the heavy moment of Mom removing her breathing mask. With her refusals of the ventilator, we stood witness to her gradual decline, saying our tearful goodbyes as she passed away.

Brix

In the sadness of losing Mom a year ago, December 8th brought another sad memory. Amid my ongoing sorrow, our cherished dog, Brix, a big French Mastiff, began showing worrisome signs. Just after his ninth birthday, he started acting differently and having trouble breathing. He was falling on walks and making a strange sound in his breath. On December 8th, the same day we lost Mom (a year later), I found myself pleading with Brix not to leave us.

The next day, a brief moment of hope arose as he appeared more lively and was enjoying Smokey Bones, as he refused regular dog food. A vet visit unveiled a big heart problem, and Brix's condition worsened quickly. My daughter, heading to Tennessee, sensed something was wrong and kissed him goodbye. Brix spent his last moments weak, vomiting, and trying to find comfort outdoors.

He mustered the strength to climb the stairs, which was a tough task for him. When my husband left for work, Brix followed him, but upon his return to the house, he settled into his bed, breathing heavily. Trying to move towards me in the kitchen, he made it halfway as he collapsed. Helplessly calling his name, I watched as he gazed at the grandfather clock. In that heartbreaking moment, he took his last breath, leaving my son and me shattered by the loss.

I pause here to ask you to hang in here as I share my journey through grief. It might seem like a lot, but I think it's important for you to really get what I've been through. To be honest, grief has become a close companion of mine. Let me be clear, being familiar with grief doesn't mean I've always handled it well. I became skilled at putting my feelings in separate boxes, which is a trick that many of us use to protect ourselves from constant pain. It's like turning down the volume on our emotions to avoid the hurt. We become accustomed to those feelings, push them away, and accidentally make healing harder. Thus, while I know grief very well from all of the losses I've endured, understanding grief and dealing with grief in the right way is not the same.

Grief Recovery

In *The Grief Recovery Handbook* by John W. James and Russell Friedman, they dive into the ways we are taught to process grief, which, let's face it, is often overshadowed by the expectation to keep moving forward, just like everything else in life. It's as if life hands you a tragedy, and you're given a specific timeframe — five weeks, maybe. Then, you're expected to "get over it" and resume your "normal" life. However, that's far from reality. Grief is a journey with ebbs and flows. Some days, you might feel okay; other days, everything seems to suck, and you're left unsure of what kind of day it'll be. Your five senses can swiftly bring back memories of the loss, acting as triggers. These triggers are particularly intense right after the loss, especially if the grief is linked to a traumatic experience. With time, healing finds a place in your heart, allowing you to inch forward. However, when individuals struggle to move on, experiencing prolonged grief becomes a mental health diagnosis outlined in *The Diagnostic and Statistical Manual of Mental Disorders, Fifth Edition, Text Revision* (DSM-5-TR). Therefore, I have a question that I'd like to pose which is: How did you learn to navigate grief?

Now, let's talk about grief in a way that hits close to home. The truth is that most of us don't handle grief the right way. We're not really taught how to deal with it, especially if we come from families that keep their emotions under wraps. As some of us learn and grow, we're becoming more aware of emotional immaturity, but it's still a bit elusive for many who haven't been educated about it. Often, grief is misinterpreted. I've shared quite a few stories about losses in my family, and I'm sure that you understand by now that grief isn't confined to just people or things. Sure, we grieve the death of a loved one. Still, grief is also the loss of a relationship, be it a friendship, family, friend, or even a pet, loss of a job, loss of health or physical abilities, loss of independence, loss of a home or significant personal possessions such as a fire, loss of a dream or expectation for the future, loss associated with important life transition like moving, empty nest, or retirement, loss of safety or security due to trauma, and the loss of identity or sense of self. Now, take a moment and pinpoint where you can identify that you are stuck in grief.

Let me paint a scenario for you. Imagine having a friend you believed to be genuine, only to discover she was undermining you behind your back. The grief you would feel wouldn't just be about losing that friendship; it extends to mourning the shattered expectations and the subsequent trust issues. Grief is not just about the person in that moment; it's about the aftermath of emotions. This is where I believe many people miss the mark. They fail to recognize certain disappointments as a form of grief, and as a result, they don't navigate the healing process effectively. It's like going to a doctor with a problem in your leg; if the doctor decides to perform surgery on your hand, it doesn't fix the issue. That's what happens when we don't address grief in the right way.

P.A.U.S.E. Method

Neglecting grief amplifies not only emotional distress but also intensifies anxiety, depression, isolation, and overall challenges in your well-being. Unresolved emotions can manifest physically and contribute to conditions like autoimmune diseases, cancer, and heart disease. It's urgent to recognize and heal from grief. Now, let me urgently guide you on how to heal by using the P.A.U.S.E. Method.

The P.A.U.S.E. method centers around the recognition that many of us frequently overlook, which is the importance of pausing to grieve authentically. It's not about setting a strict time frame for grief; instead, it's about embracing the genuine process without the pressure of rushing or delaying it.

- P - Pause when you feel overwhelmed by emotion. Take some deep breaths to calm your nervous system before reacting or making decisions.

- A - Allow the emotions to surface. Don't try to suppress them. Cry if you need to cry. Find healthy ways to express what you are feeling.

- U - Understand that your grief is normal and necessary. Be patient and compassionate with yourself as you mourn.

- S - Self-care is important right now. Make sure you get enough sleep, nutrition, hydration, movement, etc. Take things slowly and don't expect too much of yourself.

- E – Exploring how you grieve. A key yet overlooked part of grief is exploring your personal process and assessing how you typically handle, cope with, and move through loss. Understanding and openly communicating your own grief responses allows loved ones to validate and support you better, which will prevent your isolation in sorrow and facilitate deeper self-comprehension.

Inviting God on Your Healing Journey

Grief hit me hard, and it brought along its buddy — Anxiety. Losing my sister, my mom, and my dog around the holidays triggered this overwhelming fear of more losses. Winter holidays, usually a time of joy with family antics and good food, turned into a time of dread. Halloween would roll around, and my heart would start acting up, anticipating the worst. I didn't want to lose anything else; I felt as though I'd already been through more than my share.

Sleep became elusive, and every night, I found myself checking my kids' locations with a message: "Please pray and be careful." It was my secret plea for them to stay indoors. Winter became my enemy, and I dreaded them driving. I'd burst into tears if I didn't get a quick response. The anxiety took a toll on me; my chest and back often ached.

Then came a dream that shook me. In the dream, I visited a doctor for a chest X-ray, and this doctor had the most advanced machine ever. He enlarged the image on a blue screen, examining my heart. The doctor, who felt like Jesus, said, "After losing your sister, mom, and dog in three consecutive years, your heart is broken, and you're carrying sadness." It hit me; I thought that I was okay but with a bit of anxiety, but I wasn't healed. The deaths of my mom, sister, and dog had shattered my heart.

Years later, healing from grief became more profound when I invited God into my journey. Sometimes, we don't even realize that grief still lingers or that we haven't dealt with it at all. I vividly remember feeling as if I'd moved on from the pain a few years after losing my sister and mom. One day, while listening to worship music, Tina crossed my mind out of the blue.

At that moment, it felt as though God was gently nudging me and saying that I held a grudge against Him. I immediately pushed back, denying it, but He calmly pointed out that I expected Him to heal Tina and for her to beat cancer. When she passed away, I became disappointed and lost faith in Him. That loss of hope made it hard for me to believe He could do anything positive in my life. It was mind-blowing.

But this is how I know God wants you to succeed in every area of your life. God doesn't want you on the struggle bus with processing your emotions.

> "Beloved, I pray that in every way you may succeed *and* prosper and be in good health [physically], just as [I know] your soul prospers [spiritually]."
>
> *3 John 2*

Conclusion

In conclusion, it's important to acknowledge that grief is a natural emotion, and trying to resist it won't make it go away. The truth is that grief can be painful and sometimes feels overwhelming. Many of us carry the weight of grief for the loss of someone or something that we lost years ago. My hope for you is that this chapter permits you to thrive, even amidst the tears that grief brings. Grief doesn't signify the end of your life, and it's crucial to allow yourself to process it. There are moments in time when human emotions occur, and you must navigate through them. As you navigate through grief, let God be your Global Positioning System (GPS). He can direct you towards the route that's best for your personal healing journey, just as a GPS guides you on the roads. Allow God to map out the way toward recovery and peace as you travel through the unfamiliar territory of loss. With Him as your spiritual GPS, you can be assured that you won't lose your way on the road to regaining hope and joy. Trust in His wisdom to chart the course towards comfort and acceptance, and remember to give yourself grace.

About the Authors

Keosha S. Edwards

Keosha Edwards is a woman driven by an unquenchable passion for people. Her journey through life has led her down diverse and enlightening paths, each offering unique lessons and experiences that have shaped her deep commitment to positively impacting the lives of those around her.

At the core of her being lies unwavering faith. She is a devoted minister dedicated to spreading love, hope, and compassion. Her faith is the guiding light that empowers her to serve her community and uplift those in need.

In addition to her role as a minister, she is a loving and devoted mother of three wonderful children. They are her most significant source of inspiration, reminding her daily of the importance of love, empathy, and resilience.

With 23 years of banking experience, Keosha possesses a deep reservoir of expertise and knowledge. Her career in banking has equipped her with a robust skill set that she applies to her professional endeavors. Additionally, her role as a licensed kinship foster mother for children within her extended family underscores her dedication to nurturing and providing support and care for her loved ones.

While attending college, Keosha continued caring for children within her family, exemplifying her dedication to her education and her loved ones. Her quest for knowledge and her desire to extend her reach in helping others have led her on a path of learning. Currently, she is pursuing a degree in Human Services. This educational journey equips her with the tools and skills to better understand and serve the community's needs.

Every day allows her to grow, learn, and serve. With a heart full of passion, faith, and a dedication to learning, she strives to create a positive impact, one person at a time, and works towards making the world a better place.

To learn more about Minister Keosha S. Edwards, please visit:

Instagram:@keoshaedwards
Facebook:@keoshaedwards

Dr. Candice P. Parker

Destined to be a Disruptor, Dr. Candice P. Parker is the lifestyle strategist and consultant you find when you know it's time to break through barriers preventing you from boldly walking into your next level of purpose and destiny. With a relentless commitment to empowering women and families, Dr. Candice passionately has guided them in conquering the challenges of life, fostering resilience, and crafting an environment of success through unwavering faith and grace.

Dr. Candice has her Doctorate degree in Theology, a master's degree in criminal justice administration and forensic psychology, a positive discipline parent educator and a Licensed Addiction Counselor. She is the Creator of "Woman Out Loud by Candice P. Parker." a movement to help Christian women like you combat the daily stressors of life by maximizing their faith, breaking unhealthy cycles, conquering transitions with grace, and creating peace within themselves and their environments. She is also the Creator and Author of "Mom Really," a faith-based book and platform for Christian moms to improve their communication and relationship with their teens and young adults. She is a 2x Best Seller for Book Collaborations: "The Purposed Woman 365 Day Devotional" and "Bounced Back on Purpose." Additionally, she is the recipient of two awards for her work empowering women, families, and entrepreneurship.

While she brings close to two decades of professional and ministry experience to the table, she also knows how to savor life's blessings. As a devoted wife, mother to three children, and a joyful grandmother, she finds fulfillment in the family. Candice currently calls the vibrant city of Columbus, Ohio, home, and anticipates the remarkable opportunities that the future holds.

To learn more about Dr. Candice P. Parker, please visit:

Website: www.womanoutloud.com
Email: support@womanoutloud.com
Instagram: @candice.p.parker
Facebook: @candicepparker
Tiktok: @candicepparker

Sherita A. Riley

Sherita is a dynamic force, balancing two worlds with grace and dedication. By day, she serves as a Group Benefits Manager, navigating the complexities of the corporate landscape with skill and precision. But beneath this professional veneer lies a compassionate soul, a Licensed Mental Health Counselor driven by a profound desire to help others heal and thrive.

Originally hailing from Hartford, Connecticut, Sherita's journey led her to the sun-drenched area of Phoenix, Arizona in 2016, where she embarked on self-discovery and transformation. Alongside her corporate responsibilities, she devotes her time and expertise to the mental health field, drawing from her healing journey to guide others toward wholeness and fulfillment.

Sherita's professional path began in the trenches of Human Services and group residential homes, where she witnessed firsthand the resilience of the human spirit amidst adversity. Here, her passion for advocacy ignited, driving her to amplify the voices of those often overlooked by society.

Armed with a Master's Degree in Human Services and counseling, Sherita now stands as a beacon of hope for adults healing the inner child while navigating the turbulent waters of trauma, anxiety, and self-doubt. Her holistic approach to healing encompasses the mind, heart, and soul, empowering her clients to reclaim their inner strength and embrace life's challenges with courage and resilience.

Outside of her counseling practice, she finds solace and joy in the company of her three beloved children—two girls and a boy—who serve as constant reminders of life's beauty and wonder. Through her unwavering commitment to both her professional career and her role as a mother, Sherita embodies the power of balance and purpose, inspiring those around her to pursue their passions with unwavering determination.

As she continues to navigate the intricate dance between her corporate duties and her calling as a Mental Health Counselor, Sherita remains steadfast in her commitment to making a meaningful difference in the lives of others. She will soon be working towards a doctorate in Clinical Psychology and beginning to build her private practice. With each passing day, she serves as a shining example of resilience, compassion, and unwavering dedication—a true testament to the transformative power of the human spirit.

To learn more about Minister Sherita A. Riley, please visit:

Tik Tok:@She_Cactus
Facebook:@SheritaRiley

Shameka L. Jones

Shameka Jones wears many hats: as a wife, the mother of three adult sons, and the grandmother of two wonderful girls. Shameka Jones distinguishes her professional journey in healthcare with a Master's in Healthcare Administration and a Bachelor's in Healthcare Management. As the founder and owner of 360 Health Transformations LLC, where she is a certified transformation coach, Shameka skillfully combines biblical principles, psychology, science, and nutrition. This comprehensive approach aims to improve physical, mental, emotional, spiritual, and financial well-being.

Shameka is a skilled Neuro-Linguistic Programming Practitioner, an ordained minister, and the best-selling co-author of "The Unchained Goddess." Currently, she holds a significant role as a Senior Manager at a Fortune 100 Healthcare Corporation, leveraging over two decades of industry experience. Her true passion, however, lies in empowering women to enhance their health and live purposeful, fulfilling lives—an ambition she passionately refers to as living "Whole and on Purpose."

Moreover, as the president and founder of the Woman Heal Thy Soul conference and an acclaimed speaker, author, and transformational coach, Shameka Jones continues to inspire and lead women toward holistic health and personal success.

To learn more and connect with Shamkea, please visit:

Facebook:@ShamekaJones
Business:@360Healthtransformations
Facebookgroup: womanhealthysoul
Instagram:@Shamekaj01 Business:@360Healthtransformations and @womanhealthysoul
Tiktok: Shamekajones360

Krystal A. Edwards

Krystal Edwards, a multi-talented individual of Caribbean descent, embodies roles as a child of God, a pastor, a mother, a wife, a daughter, and a sister with a deep passion for serving others. With over 14 years of experience in human services, she is the founder of Grace Valley Clinical Services LLC and a Licensed Professional Counselor.

Having graduated with a Bachelor's in Psychology from the University Of Hartford in 2009 and earned a Master's Degree in Human Services with a concentration in Clinical

Counseling at Post University in 2014, Krystal has dedicated her career to providing behavioral health services to adolescents, adults, and individuals with disabilities.

Her professional journey includes diverse roles as a Behavioral Specialist, Social Worker Investigator, Therapist, Mentor, and Vocational Counselor at esteemed organizations like New Hope Manor, REM CT Community Services, The Department Of Children and Families, and The Department of Aging and Disabilities. In 2022, she established Grace Valley Clinical Services —a private practice rooted in her faith and commitment to community service.

As the owner of a private practice, Krystal ensures personalized care and support for individuals by staying updated on the latest research and therapeutic techniques. Her diverse skill set, unwavering passion for helping others, and unique blend of expertise, spirituality, and relatability make her a trusted guide for those seeking transformation and fulfillment in mental health and personal development.

Krystal also serves as a pastor at The Remnant Church of God in Hartford, CT, offering spiritual guidance and support to those in need. She is a Christian and mental health content creator who utilizes her platform as a social media influencer to disseminate positivity, inspiration, and mental health awareness to a broad audience. As she embarks on this new chapter as an author, she adds another prestigious title to her impressive repertoire, showcasing that she is just starting her impactful journey.

To learn more about Pastor Krystal Edwards, please visit:

Tiktok: @CreatedbyGodCT
Instagram: @GraceValleyLLC
Facebook: @GraceValleyClinicalServices
Website: GraceValleyClinicalServices.com

Dr. Janell Jones

Dr. Janell Jones is an esteemed TEDx Speaker, certified life coach, national and international best-selling author, and licensed clinical therapist. With a profound dedication to personal growth and empowerment, Dr. Jones embarked on a transformative journey that would shape her career and impact countless lives.

Driven by her passion for uplifting others, Dr. Jones founded Melanin Grace Publishing, LLC, a pioneering publishing company committed to amplifying diverse voices and stories. Through Melanin Grace Publishing, she has provided a platform for marginalized voices to be heard, fostering inclusivity and representation within the literary world.

As the host of "Empowerment TV" on YouTube, Dr. Jones shares her insights and experiences, inspiring women from all walks of life to pursue their passions and dreams relentlessly. Through candid conversations, practical advice, and motivational content, she encourages viewers to unlock their full potential and live authentically.

Dr. Jones's expertise extends to coaching women, helping them clarify their goals, overcome obstacles, and monetize their life's purpose. With a personalized approach rooted in empathy and understanding, she guides her clients towards fulfillment and success, empowering them to create meaningful and impactful lives.

Beyond her professional endeavors, Dr. Jones is deeply committed to philanthropy and social change. As the founder of Beauty in Mahogany, Inc., a non-profit organization dedicated to empowering girls of color, she provides essential support and resources to help them build self-esteem, confidence, and leadership skills. Through mentorship programs, workshops, and community outreach initiatives, Dr. Jones is actively shaping the next generation of leaders and changemakers.

Furthermore, Dr. Jones leads the You Factory program, a transformative platform designed to help individuals heal from past traumas and cultivate resilience. Through a combination of therapeutic techniques, coaching, and self-discovery exercises, she empowers participants to overcome their challenges and move forward with clarity and purpose.

Dr. Janell Jones's story is a powerful testament to the transformative potential of resilience, determination, and unwavering commitment to making a difference. Through her work, she continues to inspire and uplift countless individuals, leaving an indelible mark on the world.

To learn more about Dr. Janell Jones, please visit:

Webiste: www.janelljonesempowers
IG: @janelljonesempowers
Facebook @janelljonesempowers
Tiktok @janelljonesempowers

Bold, Booked, and Balanced membership:
www.boldbookedandbalanced.com

For The You Factory Program that combines healing and purpose, please go to: www.theyoufactory.com

An Exclusive Offering

Here's a Little Something Extra for You. We believe that when a woman heals herself, she heals generations. That's a profound truth, and we wish to be present with you every step of this meaningful journey. To that end, we are providing you with complimentary worksheets including a Self-Reflection Journey and Embrace Self-Assessments.

These will help you identify where you currently stand on your path of healing and how to continue progressing. Consider it a gentle encouragement from us to sustain the positive momentum after completing the book. Let us continue walking this transformative path together, fostering growth that can impact lives across generations.

https://bit.ly/womanhealthysoul

Resources

American Psychological Association. (2024). Mindfulness. Retrieved from https://www.apa.org/topics/mindfulness#:~:text=Mindfulness%20is%20awareness%20of%20one's,judging%20or%20reacting%20to%20them.

BibleGateway. (n.d.). 2 Corinthians 10:4-5 (New Living Translation). Retrieved February 22, 2024, from www.biblegateway.com.

BibleGateway. (n.d.). Galatians 5:22-23 (New Living Translation). Retrieved February 22, 2024, from www.biblegateway.com.

BibleGateway. (n.d.). John 14:27 (New Living Translation). Retrieved February 22, 2024, from www.biblegateway.com.

BibleGateway. (n.d.). Matthew 6:28-29 (New Living Translation). Retrieved February 22, 2024, from www.biblegateway.com.

BibleGateway. (n.d.). Psalm 46:10 (New Living Translation). Retrieved February 22, 2024, from www.biblegateway.com.

BibleGateway. (n.d.). Psalms 139:14 (New Living Translation). Retrieved February 22, 2024, from www.biblegateway.com.

BibleGateway. (n.d.). Romans 8:28 (New Living Translation). Retrieved February 22, 2024, from www.biblegateway.com.

BibleGateway. (n.d.). Romans 8:31 (English Standard Version). Retrieved February 22, 2024, from www.biblegateway.com.

BibleGateway. (n.d.). Romans 8:37 (New Living Translation). Retrieved February 22, 2024, from www.biblegateway.com.

BibleGateway. (n.d.). Romans 12:2 (New Living Translation). Retrieved February 22, 2024, from www.biblegateway.com.

Chowdhury, R. (2019). What Is Emotional Resilience. Retrieved from https://positivepsychology.com/emotional-resilience/

Covenant Counseling Services. (2024). Being Whole: 21 Days to Overcoming Relational Trauma. Retrieved April 10, 2024, from https://thecovenantcounselor.com/

James, J. W., & Friedman, R. (n.d.). The Grief Recovery Handbook: The Action Program for Moving Beyond Death, Divorce, and Other Losses including Health, Career, and Faith. HarperCollins.

www.ingramcontent.com/pod-product-compliance
Lightning Source LLC
Chambersburg PA
CBHW030556080526
44585CB00012B/389